EXPOSED

A MEMOIR

an unexpected journey from fear to freedom

NANCY SLOMOWITZ

N3 PUBLICATIONS, LLC
DARNESTOWN, MD

Published by
N3 Publications, LLC
Darnestown, MD

   Publisher's Cataloging-in-Publication Data
   Slomowitz, Nancy.

   Exposed : an unexpected journey from fear to freedom / Nancy
   Slomowitz. – Darnestown, MD. : N3 Publications, LLC., 2017.

   p. ; cm.

   ISBN13: 978-0-9848408-4-7

   1. Slomowitz, Nancy. 2. Women executives—United States—
   Biography. 3. Businesswomen—United States—Biography.
   4. Success in business. I. Title.

   HD6054.4.U6 S56 2017
   658.409082—dc23   2016917972

Project coordination by Jenkins Group, Inc.
www.BookPublishing.com

Interior design by Brooke Camfield

Printed in the United States of America
21   20   19   18   17   •   5   4   3   2   1

*To the hidden masters who appeared at just the right time
to guide me on this amazing journey.*

Contents

Strength does not come from winning.
Your struggles develop your strengths.
When you go through hardships and
decide not to surrender, that is strength.

—MOHANDAS GANDHI

Foreword

To an extent, we all live in glass houses, understanding our vulnerabilities, insecurities and struggles. But rarely do we throw the proverbial stones through our own windowpanes, publicly shattering what we've built, exposing ourselves in near complete nakedness to any who would gawk.

But by leaving herself "Exposed," Washington DC entrepreneur Nancy Slomowitz does just that! And if you are wondering why an otherwise perfectly sane, middle-aged, highly successful businesswoman would pose in her "unmentionables" for a book cover, you are not alone.

Nancy herself admits, "To stand in front of the world in my underwear is embarrassing!" Indeed, other than highly paid models, who does this?

The raw, coarse and unvarnished answers are in the pages beyond the visually metaphorical hook of the cover.

Exposed takes you on a familiar journey that many people share—childhood dreams diverted by life's realities, often leading to years of somnolently plodding along, both intellectually and creatively—to hopefully experiencing a reawakening.

The familiarity ends there, because Nancy has stripped her mind, heart, and soul to their skivvies with brutal self-examination and honesty. It is neither mea culpa nor "woe is me!" Quite the contrary, *Exposed* offers a public exploration of a private human struggle, intended to encourage you to do your own internal audit—strip yourself to the core, find your foundation, and rebuild from there.

Rather than an unctuous, pontificating swing at pop culture self-help, *Exposed* is a painfully personal, public self-audit. As a young woman, Nancy abandoned her dreams on a shelf for another calling. And while deftly navigating the challenges she faced as a young female entrepreneur in a shark-infested, male-dominated town, by any external measure, Nancy accomplishes sweet success. But eventually she finds it bitter and soulless. And at a time when she should be relishing the rewards of her nose-to-the-grindstone existence, she chucks it all to recapture her youthful dreams.

Exposed is not a glamorous tale; instead, it's rife with the realities of risk, heartache, and the thrill of victory and the agony of defeat. There's a targeted critique of the fashion industry, its homogenization of women in the workplace, and a healthy dollop of government incompetence. Surprisingly, those seemingly disparate, unwieldy tentacles fit together awkwardly but neatly.

Nancy approaches all with the mind-set that "Sunlight is the best disinfectant."

Even as innocent kids, most never want to be caught in our underwear. Nancy has volunteered to do so, hoping that by shining light on her own human struggle, you might be inspired to do the same!

Jim Forbes, President
Jim Forbes Voice, Inc.

Introduction

By midlife, I had put together the kind of life most outside observers would judge as near perfect. I had "made it." I was one of the self-made people who had reached financial independence, creating something useful and valuable out of virtually nothing. I had built and maintained a successful company that delivered a quality service and that gave meaningful employment to many. My husband and I lived in a beautifully restored historic home in the suburbs that brought us great joy. We had good friends. I had a great dog. I had everything I wanted—or so it seemed.

For a long time, I believed the illusion was the real thing. Once I realized I was living in a "comfortably numb" but totally unfulfilled state, I had to face my fears and find the courage to start doing something about it. I had to take a breath and dig deep—jumping into unknown territory is a scary thing. In the end, I decided to strap on my helmet, get ready for the wild ride ahead, and take that leap of faith. I knew that deconstructing everything I had created to support my old belief system was a difficult but unavoidable step in building a meaningful new life. Things begin to unfold very quickly after you break the glass and sound the fire alarm.

Those closest to me had no idea what I was up to. In retrospect, even I didn't realize the scope and magnitude of what lay ahead. But I was only practicing the heart of what had made me successful in my profession—following my instinct and intuition even when my life choices strayed far away from conventional thinking.

Why was I so unfulfilled in the first place, and why did it take so long for me to realize it? In hindsight, the answers may make perfect sense, but that's not how life works. Instead, getting to the ultimate truth and unraveling what went wrong to set it right put me on a twisting and unpredictable journey.

I've written this book in real time, getting the story down as it happened. Oddly enough, you will see that some of the most difficult things I faced, and that brought me the most anguish in the moment, ended up becoming the greatest blessings.

I share this with the hope that my story will help you, the reader, stay open to all the possibilities that exist in any given situation, including difficult and seemingly hopeless circumstances. I hope you will see how the most rewarding opportunities may unexpectedly emerge out of the things that don't go our way. These are the "course corrections" (not failures) and other bumps in the road we all encounter.

Our first step in recognizing that we have a real problem often requires us to turn the mirror on ourselves. The consequences of doing so can unleash a painful cleanup of our emotional baggage, a task in itself that deters many people from even starting down this path. Talk about skeletons in the closet! Mine was the place where many difficult truths had been stored away. It is the storage space for many of those "here we go again" behaviors that we know are wrong but that we can't seem to help ourselves avoid. Once the process is set in motion, the journey can take you to unpredictable and amazing places, as long as you maintain your courage and keep moving forward. For me, there was no turning back. Returning to my life as I once knew it was not an option.

This is a story about redemption from a safe but unfulfilling life and about finding a true source of fulfillment and joy within. Whether we've made it or are barely hanging on, the problems we share in modern Western society come from the same core: a disheartening absence of passion that results from our failure to fully embrace and maximize our true gifts. Ignored, discouraged, and thwarted, our dormant talents that we've failed to tap into can cut us off from our highest forms of creative energy and leave us tired, spiritually empty, and defeated.

This book gives thanks to the many remarkable people who appeared at the right moments to guide and teach me and to help me open doors of opportunity and growth. Whether it came from a more obvious source like a parent, or from brief encounters with strangers, none of it seems accidental. Things do happen for a reason.

CHAPTER 1

Bearers of Gifts

I could argue that the curiously random sequence of events was actually inevitable that early spring day of late 2012 in the Washington, DC neighborhood of Georgetown. I had made plans to meet my friend Anthony for lunch right after a hair appointment.

"I'm going to walk around and come back," Anthony told me, impatient that my styling session was taking longer than usual. Anthony is my closest friend and confidant, a charismatic jewelry designer I had met years before at a trunk show. Ours is a provocative friendship. Because we're always truthful with each other, we can get under each other's skin and become infuriated with one another for days or weeks on end.

There's a silver lining in it, however, because it forces us to face and resolve some inner issue that is limiting our potential. The long-term personal growth we achieve outweighs the short-term pain of our disagreements. I know it may sound crazy, but it's like Anthony and I are mirrors of each other.

The salon was our agreed upon meeting place prior to heading over for lunch at a nearby restaurant called Clyde's. It was raining outside that day. Umbrella in hand, Anthony left the salon to explore the nearby shops and escape the noise from the hairdryers and the noxious smells.

Fifteen minutes later, he came back as excited as a child asking for a treat. "Oh my God, there's a psychic around the corner," he said. "I really, *really* want to go!"

"Okay, let's do it," I told him. Turnabout is fair play. Because of the wait at the salon, I could sit for a while in the psychic's office while he got his fortune told, I thought. We weren't so hungry that lunch couldn't wait.

It turned out there were actually two fortune-tellers in the neighborhood. The nearest one was too busy, and we decided not to wait. We went around the next corner to another one he had found on his walk. The sign in the window read, *Psychic Readings by Cassidy*. We laughed, carrying our folded, wet umbrellas up two very steep and narrow flights of stairs, getting out of breath as we reached the top. Ringing the doorbell, Anthony suddenly realized that his parking meter was about to expire.

"I'm not going back down those stairs," I told him, still recovering from the climb. "I'm staying here."

"Then why don't *you* go in until I come back," he suggested.

I had not the slightest interest in having a reading by Cassidy or anyone else. The clear understanding was that Anthony was going to have his session, and I was going to wait. But the doorbell had been rung, and I was standing there alone with a wet umbrella and raincoat. I would simply have to tell Cassidy or her staff person that Anthony would be back in a few minutes and that I was just a friend who was there to wait for him while he had his reading.

The very proposition of seeing a psychic brought back ridiculous and less than pleasant childhood memories of being dragged along by my mother to palm readers. What my mother loved to hear was the stuff of schoolgirl fantasies; for example, how she was going to meet the suave villain Victor Newman from the soap opera *The Young and the Restless* and be whisked off to his palatial estate.

On one occasion, my mother got the palm reader to look at my hand. "A long life with three kids," that psychic told me. The part about the kids would turn out to be as wrong as wrong can be. Since that time, I'd had no interest to ever go again.

"Okay, I'll do it," I told Anthony, surprising myself with my response. I would meet with the psychic. It would pass the time until he came back. We were both in that "let's go, it will be so funny" mind-set. I told myself the amount of money it would cost would be worth some good laughs afterward at lunch.

Just seconds after Anthony disappeared, Cassidy came to the door. She was not your stereotypical fortune-teller clad in New Age adornments. Instead, her outward appearance called little attention to herself. She looked more like one of my friends or coworkers. She was of average build and appeared to be about a decade younger than me.

Once inside her front door, Cassidy got down to business and handed me a paper with a menu of options. "What would you like? Tarot cards, palm reading?"

"Nah."

"Why don't you do a basic reading for $90?"

"That's perfect. That's fine."

With that, Cassidy led me through some French doors to her inner sanctum, a room no bigger than a closet. Inside was barely space for two chairs and a glass table, all of which looked like garden furniture. On the table were a bunch of crystals. A colorful tapestry with geometric shapes was hanging from a rod on the wall.

She called me into the closet-like place, and before I could get comfortable, she reached underneath the table and took out a credit card machine. After swiping my card, she gave me one of the crystals from the table to hold. She then asked me my birthday.

Cassidy didn't seem to move into some altered state to perform her reading. She just closed her eyes for a few seconds of silence. As she began to speak, the very first words that came out of her mouth were, "You are a very talented writer." That was an interesting insight. Some months before, I had published my first book, *Work Zone Madness, Surviving and Rising Above Workplace Dysfunction,* and it was now available on Amazon.

"You're a very creative person, but you're in a business capacity." Repeating for emphasis, Cassidy elaborated, "You're a very creative person, but you've suppressed that for many years."

Not stopping there, she began to hammer away at my personal life. Some of my personal relationships had fallen in line to support this unfulfilling existence, she explained, and they had helped tighten the stifling stranglehold that my current life had on me. "And what is it with this marriage? You're in a marriage, but it's not a marriage. What's all this about? You've buried that creative side of yourself, but it's about to come back."

Cassidy was venturing into a far deeper and hidden aspect of my life, prying a lid off some undeniable truths. The truth about the marriage part hit especially hard. Rick was my best friend and a wonderful partner in our business, but what she picked up on was years of a relationship existing on automatic pilot. All of this could have been disturbing, but I found it enlightening and accurate.

In fact, sitting there in the little room listening to Cassidy, I had an overwhelming sensation of astonishment. I had always been a great actress, award winning at mastering the art of the poker face both at work and in my private life. I didn't show emotion to people, period. But Cassidy was able to see right through me. That she totally "got me" was the most unexpected thing of all. How was it that no one had ever understood me so well before? It was encouraging, exciting—and unsettling.

There was very little else of the twenty minutes we spent together that I remember or need to remember. She had said enough. I had walked into her little closet thinking I had as close to a perfect life as imaginable, and I left thunderstruck and daunted at how I could have deluded myself for so long. Borrowing from the Pink Floyd song, I had spent my life up to that point in the state of being "comfortably numb." When I got up from her chair, I was suddenly *un*comfortably numb. It was also immediately clear that there was no going back to my old ways, no matter what it would take to change.

From the beginning, I had been a very unhappy and troubled child who from the deepest core rebelled at any efforts by others to impose conformity. I was, according to my parents, the "broke the mold when they made you" poster child. The same factors that drove me often to despair and nearly to the brink of suicide mercifully found a more constructive outlet as I grew into adulthood. Simply put, being so rebellious made me far more aware and far less accepting of the stifling conventions society creates for orderliness and control. This translated into an advantage that would eventually bring me great success in business. To me, that tired cliché of "thinking outside the box" came as easy as cake. Throughout my financial career, I enjoyed the challenge of identifying the hidden errors buried in a sea of numbers, successfully finding new ways to create order out of the problems and chaos I uncovered.

If career success and financial independence had been enough to produce my contentment and happiness, then what happened that particular morning would have had no impact on my life whatsoever. At most, it would have provided an offbeat story to tell a friend and then to quickly forget. Instead, this lark of a visit to a clairvoyant became nothing short of a catalyst for what I call my

"Second Act." It ultimately took a mold-breaking sledgehammer to the existential midlife dissatisfaction I faced: "Do I really want to go on living the rest of my life like this?"

Anthony was waiting for me outside on the landing when I came out of Cassidy's lair. A couple of "oh my Gods" was all I had time to tell him as he passed by me on his way in for his own reading. I took a seat to wait for him at the small table that was outside her door. My mind went through gymnastics trying to make sense of what had just happened. Despite the undeniable nature of what she brought forward, suspicion and doubt were natural places to go. "How could she possibly have been so dead accurate?"

Just to be sure she was legit, I went through a mental checklist. No, there was nothing in my appearance that could have given her any clues. I was not dressed in business attire nor did I have a briefcase in hand like had I come from work. I was dressed casually in my weekend wear. Could she have done a Google search? No, that was impossible. I obviously hadn't made the appointment in advance; I'd walked in off the street. She had no idea who I was.

Twenty minutes or so later, Anthony came out with a similar deer-in-the-headlights look. At Clyde's bistro, we gave each other highly edited accounts of what Cassidy had told us. It was all so personal, the kind of stuff you didn't want to admit to yourself let alone talk to anyone else about. I needed time to absorb it all, but there was more to it than that.

There are some experiences in life, especially things that touch a spiritual dimension, that you want to keep undisturbed in a pure state. The minute you start talking about it, you run the risk that the mystical effect will begin to evaporate. There's also the way people always try to put an intellectual spin on things that really defy logical explanation. Sharing that kind of experience can end up cheapening the whole thing.

In the days that followed, the effect of my reading with Cassidy transitioned from surprise and excitement to more of a feeling of devastation. The cold water she threw on my carefully constructed facade became more disturbing the more I thought about it. Standing back, I saw how it had all worked so beautifully to achieve all the goals, the now shallow career goals, I had set for myself. Suddenly all of that had evaporated.

I was an emotional wreck, but I weathered it, knowing the pain was a kind of detox. I also knew I needed outside help. Friends could not do it—no one in my circle was in a position to help me. They had all done what I had unconsciously asked them to do—support and foster my state of numbness. There was a lot to unravel and work through, so I decided to start working with a psychotherapist named David. He had taken over the practice from his late father, whom Rick and I had seen for couple's therapy decades earlier.

In the weeks that turned into months that followed, we honed in on the decisions I had made about my life some twenty-eight years earlier when my father died. Many of those decisions, I learned, had been the right ones at that time. Giving up my creative dreams for a financially stable job made sense at a time when I needed to be the anchor for my family. But the critical realization was that I was no longer stuck in the 1980s.

While my life circumstances were radically different now, I was still acting from crisis mode, sticking to the decisions and choices I had made back then. David helped me understand that I didn't have to live that way any longer. This helped break through my internal deadlock and showed me how it was possible to make changes and get myself back on the right path.

Rick attended many of the sessions with me, as we tried to understand and work through our issues. I learned that conventional therapy could only go so far in cracking through the layers of my psyche. I was a good talker and poured out my feelings, but eventually I hit a wall. After several months, the therapy had gone as far as it could take me, and we called it a day. I needed to go deeper into my soul for answers. And I would.

CHAPTER 2

Old Days

Once I committed to this crazy act of reinventing myself, the process seemed unstoppable, moving into high gear on its own steam. I had taken the first big step of freeing myself from the fear that held me back. That was no easy task. For as successful as I had been as a businesswoman, I still suffered from severe, childhood-rooted insecurities that I did everything I could to mask. Once liberated from that, my attitude began to shift and my protective shell began to chip and crumble.

On this front, the story of Jason Scheff is a quirky example of how, when we are truly ready for change, it will find us in one form or another (and quite often bringing with it something that far exceeds our expectations). The tie-in to Jason was on the surface simple and straightforward. It began with the fact that I was a fan of his band, the legendary rock and jazz-fusion group Chicago. Jason is the group's lead singer and bassist.

You have to understand that music is not a casual interest for me; instead, it's a deep passion. It has always been there, especially when things got tough. I had been plagued for decades by a childhood of being misunderstood and repressed. I was the quintessential screaming child who nobody listened to. Music became the only place where I found safe haven, where songs and lyrics reached out to me and validated what I was feeling. This was especially true about Chicago. From the time I first heard the song, "25 or 6 to 4," when I was in the sixth grade, I became obsessed with their music and had to buy every one of their albums. I felt like they were speaking directly to me through their songs.

My childhood love for music never found expression in mastering an instrument or learning how to sing. I had taught myself to play the basics of the organ when I was eight years old and even played in a recital. But the minute my parents arranged formal lessons for me, I didn't want to do it anymore. I so hated being regimented. Since I didn't play and I couldn't sing, listening to pop songs that expressed what I was feeling inside became my personal therapy during troubling times in my life. They gave me a safety valve of release that kept me from exploding.

The best example of how music literally saved my life happened when my world came crashing down on me at age fifteen. Central to this story is our family dog, Go-go, a chocolate-brown toy poodle that my parents had bought for me to help me cope with my emotional problems. And the dog did just that; Go-go was truly a therapy dog before they coined the phrase. I felt he was the only being in the family who really understood me. When Go-go was about seven years old, my parents took him to the vet to have his teeth cleaned. Perhaps they gave him too much anesthesia, but the dog that came home that day was never the same.

We lived in a two-level house with a staircase that went down to a fenced backyard. One day, shortly after his vet appointment, I let Go-go out. He seemed at the time to be recovering from the vet experience. I called out the dog's name, but he wouldn't come up, so I went downstairs and got him. It seemed right after that moment that his health went into a steep decline. He wouldn't eat, and he could barely lift up his head. My dad started taking him back and forth to the vet. We were worried about Go-go, but we thought he would bounce back.

One morning, I woke up and heard my parents crying in the other room. I panicked thinking that Go-go had gotten worse. When I saw my parents, they told me that they had put him to sleep that morning. I remember feeling so upset with them. Why didn't they let me say good-bye? My dad made things worse without really intending to because he was crying when he told me the news. "I went down there and opened the door to his room this morning, and it was just awful," he sobbed, without giving me any details. He had apparently found Go-go in very bad shape, shaking and very obviously nearing the end of his life.

Compounding matters, my parents, despite their emotional response in the moment, told me later to "just get over it." Like so many other children, the loss of a pet was my first encounter with death. I had no outlet for my grief. (Attitudes were different then, in an era where, in the event of a death of a human friend or relative, therapy and grief counseling were rare). It was certainly one of the worst days of my childhood. Far worse, my father also started getting seriously ill at about that time.

While all of this was happening, Chicago had just come out with a new album entitled *Chicago VIII*. There was one song on it, "Old Days," that I really liked. I can picture it like it was yesterday, sitting on the floor, earphones plugged into the portable record player (the kind that looks like it's inside a suitcase) and playing that one song over and over again.

The song's nostalgic lyrics, referencing good times gone away, became more meaningful to me as I worked through the grieving process. In fact, my connection with the group Chicago and their songs would play out for me over many decades. It was my therapy, helping me deal with my issues and find expression for my feelings. In the late 1980s, as I dealt with my father's illness and death, another song, "Will You Still Love Me," (which happened to be Jason's first song as lead singer of the group) resonated deeply. Its lyric, "Just say you'll love me stay around, you'll never be alone," struck to the core of the loneliness, emptiness, and devastating void that I felt from my father's death.

People around me knew that whenever these particular Chicago songs were playing, in concert or on the radio, I'd be riveted to my seat in a kind of Zen-like state. They recognized how the songs helped me cope with things in some secret way.

CHAPTER 3

The Seacret

In keeping with my deep connection to the group over the years, I signed up for all of Chicago's online fan clubs, including an online newsletter called *Scheffland*, which was about "everything Jason." One day, I opened a group message from Jason to his subscribers. The email began by telling about his family and how happy he was to be going on an Asian tour to some of his favorite cities in the world. Then he cut to the chase. Jason had a product he was endorsing, and he had a proposition he wanted us to consider:

> *And lastly . . . people have been hinting in a subtle way (and sometimes not so subtle), "Jason, you need to moisturize . . ." and now I'm in Utah where it's ULTRA dry! So some pals turned me on to a skin care line called Seacret. It's the "Dead Sea Minerals" skin care line that's been in the malls in the kiosks . . . Been using it for 6 weeks now and I can't believe how I lived without it. SO, I loved it so much I added it to*

> *my product line I market! Yup . . . Sheffy is a Seacret*
> *Agent! Haaaaaa.*

The rest of the email continued a pitch for readers to try the product, and better still, become a "Preferred Customer," which meant signing up for an automatic monthly order. There were all sorts of incentives on pricing, upgrades, and redeemable points for free products. An exclusive four-song sampler of his music ramped up to an eight-song sampler and, lastly, to a personal phone call from Jason. These were offered to encourage a higher level of participation. It meant getting more deeply involved in selling the products to friends, family, and associates. Was it strange to get such a "but wait, there's more" marketing pitch from a rock star? Whatever hesitation I might have had quickly dissolved for three big reasons. First of all, I am an unapologetic skin-care junkie. With sensitive, problematic skin, I am always on the prowl for great products. If down to my last dollar, I would spend it to feed my skin before my belly. If Jason felt so strongly about Seacret, I was in to at least try it. Had he been hawking Ginsu knives or tighter abs, on the other hand, the matter would have come to a dead stop.

The second reason I signed on was the incentive. Getting the special CD was really great, but what I wanted most was the phone call.

The last reason was one of those gut reactions, something hard to put into words. There were some intriguing and admirable qualities about Jason and his energy that I could feel in between the lines of his sales pitch, plus there were the songs I'd admired for so long. So I reached out. Over the coming days and weeks, the emails got progressively more personalized, and the promised phone call was coming soon:

Hello Nancy! Greetings from Osaka! . . . As per my October Promotion I believe I owe you a phone call! Just give me a phone number to reach you and I'll give you a shout when I get back to the states. That will be in the first week in November. And let me know once you've tried your Seacret products! I can't wait to hear! Your friend, Jason.

As promised, I got back to him with my initial test results from the using the products: "Wow!!! This product line gets top marks from me—5 stars!!! . . . Love it so far—thank you for including me in this journey. I am really getting excited about this!!! Nancy"

"Wonderful. As my mentor has told me, the right folks will all of a sudden start appearing . . . eerie how true that is! Have a great one Nancy! Greetings from Jakarta! Jason"

I was probably the third person of about a dozen or more from his list who signed on. I was also beginning to learn the unfolding truth of what his mentor meant.

Jason was still in Asia when I got a follow-up email about setting a time for the phone call. Rick and I were just walking in the front door from our twenty-fifth wedding anniversary dinner. I'd had a couple of glasses of champagne, so I was feeling no pain and especially no nervousness that I might have otherwise felt at the prospect of this conversation.

"Why not do it now," I wrote back to him.

"Do you have Skype," he asked.

"I'll be right with you," I texted back. A few seconds later, he popped up on my screen. I didn't have time to think about it or get anxious. Almost immediately, he was transformed in my mind far beyond just being the lead singer for Chicago. We connected big time and talked about everything for two and a half hours! It was

dumbfounding, this amazing cathartic thing, that here was someone who just totally seemed to get me right from the beginning,
and vice versa.

In this conversation and in our follow-up calls and emails, I
also learned what Jason's actual Seacret payoff was. He told me
point-blank that he had a great musical gig, but he knew it wasn't
going to last forever. "I was one of the lucky ones," he wrote. "I got
into the music business early. But it's not a good gamble anymore if
you are depending on supporting yourself by earning income in the
industry. This Seacret opportunity can be as simple as consuming
a product we already use, together, to create an additional income
stream."

Gone were the days when artists made a mint from selling
albums. The Internet, iTunes, and the illegal copying of music had
brought this about. The only surefire way to make money is from
concert tours. Jason, in contrast, wanted to set an example of an
alternative career other performers could do in their downtime.

What was also novel to me was his idea of building this new
relationship with his fans while he was still in his current gig. He
didn't need to wait until his performing days were over. His thinking was: *One gig doesn't have to end for the other to begin. Why not
cultivate that relationship with people in your current network to help
take you to the next place?* This was probably the last thing I would
have thought of applying to my own situation. But I would learn
to think that way.

Jason's whole approach was very different from mine, and that's
what I liked. *This is a really smart guy,* I thought. *He has a lot going
on inside, a lot of energy and drive.* If he were an egomaniac, then I
would have just been another number to him. But he treated his
fans like they were friends and soon-to-be colleagues.

What I was beginning to tap into through Jason was even better
than getting great skin care or insights into the music business.

He also started telling me about his life coach, who had actually introduced him to the possibilities of multilevel marketing (which the coach called "relationship marketing"). With it came some remarkably effective tools for personal transformation. Jason's guru and upline (the person above him in Seacret's sales organization chart) was a former construction worker and ex-Amway salesman, named Craig Holiday. Another unlikely and disguised master was about to show up in my life—the hidden secret in Seacret.

As I stated in the beginning, the genie was now out of the bottle. I was about to cast aside a lot of my old, outdated, and delusional self-perceptions that had been holding me back.

CHAPTER 4

Jumping In

"*Invitation—and yes, this is NUTS.*" This was the subject line/ disclaimer on my email blast of a Seacret event to friends, coworkers, and colleagues. What soon followed is another testimony—perhaps the most quirky and unexpected of all—of how the right people and the right circumstances come together at just the right moment to help us take that next big leap forward.

> "Please join me for a very special Seacret Spa Party this Saturday, November 10th from 12:00–2:00 p.m., hosted at my home with my new partner, Jason Scheff, the lead singer of my favorite rock group, Chicago. We recently formed a very exciting partnership and I am inviting my closest friends and family to attend the pre-launch of our new venture!!"

A spa party is where agents introduce the Seacret business opportunity and demonstrate the skin-care products in small groups.

As a new agent, I had just received my starter kit from Seacret HQ, which included information on how to conduct a spa party/event. The initial event is usually intended for close friends and family, cohosted with your sponsor. In my case that was Jason.

The invitation mentioned that women should bring extra makeup for touch-ups before they went home. But it did not go so far as to flaunt a once-in-a-lifetime chance to have facial cleansing milk applied to their skin by a real rock star. I hoped my strong reputation from throwing great annual office parties for many on the email list would encourage any doubters to RSVP quickly.

The disclaimer at the beginning meant I had anticipated the raised eyebrows, the "what in the hell is she doing?" No doubt the invitation was greeted with a flood of rush-to-judgment reactions. "Why is our colleague/boss/client doing this? Is there something we don't know? Are things getting tight? Isn't that kind of thing beneath her? What's next, rolling out the latest Tupperware or spilling dirt on the carpet to demonstrate an incredibly awesome vacuum cleaner?" Even that I was inviting them over to my home was out of character. I was so guarded and protective of my privacy that many people I had worked alongside of for years had never been inside my front door.

To family members and others who had been close friends for decades, none of this came as a great shock—unexpected, maybe, but surprise, no. They knew I was high-energy and impulsive. I had a history of immersing myself in intense projects inside, and outside, of work, such as setting up a nonprofit educational charity in my father's name, the Gilbert Slomowitz Foundation, or producing a documentary film on the stress-relieving benefits of meditation in the workplace. "Nancy selling skin care" was not so out of character given all the motley jobs that I'd had in my youth, which were fueled by my desire to be fulfilled and independent.

All of these up-from-the-bootstraps experiences—being the waitress at the Red Banjo pizzeria who got the orders wrong but still got good tips, working as a young real estate agent eager for commissions, or biding my time as an eager-to-gain-experience temp in all sorts of businesses. I'd held many nitty-gritty apprenticeships. Among other benefits, these jobs offered me invaluable insights about the real world of business and of human behavior that I continue to draw from to this day. Still, it must have seemed odd to them for a successful CEO with a demanding day job to moonlight! I'm sure it made many people scratch their heads in wonderment.

But it was a no-brainer for me. Entering Jason's world of "relationship marketing" was unquestionably a rewarding and interesting concept, something new to add to my toolbox. Contrary to what others might have believed, it didn't feel like a huge commitment. It was fun. I was only too eager to branch out of the day-to-day routine of my corporate work and try something new. I was bored and frustrated, and sitting on the couch watching TV in the evenings was not going to help anything. I thought, *Here's an opportunity that has presented itself to you. It has some really interesting elements. Maybe it won't work out, but give it a try.* And whatever it was, it was lighting up something inside of me.

It was also crazy how quickly everything was happening. Two weeks after that first Skype conversation from Osaka, I was picking Jason up at the airport for the spa party. During that ride to my house, I took a call and introduced Jason on speakerphone to a friend. "Strap on your helmet," he warned Jason, which wasn't a knock on my driving, but more of a commentary on the unpredictable ride of being part of my world.

Doing this "cultivation event" was part of the commitment to my new labor of love, an initiation of sorts. What sweetened the deal was that my "upline"—i.e., Jason—was required under the terms of Seacret to do the party with me, his mentee. Chicago had booked a concert date in the area, so he had told me, "I'm coming in early to do your spa party with you."

I have a renovated barn next to my house. We had set up our guests inside at a large table, served them food and drinks, and then had them apply a variety of facial cleansers and creams.

The spa party went well despite some obvious challenges, especially our lack of experience. I was a first-timer, but I didn't realize that Jason was a rookie with such events as well. To say we fumbled through it would be diplomatic.

I didn't know what half the products were. Jason dropped the flipchart on the floor in the middle of his talk and clung to his written notes throughout for dear life. Despite all of that, our guests enjoyed themselves and were impressed by the immediate effect of the products on their skin. The party had lived up to the hype in the invitation.

On the business side of things, the event was a great success. Almost everyone who tried the product that afternoon experienced the difference right away and bought into Seacret subscriptions. The sincerity and conviction that both Jason and I felt to the core about what we were selling shone through and probably made the bumbling, seat-of-the-pants presentation all the more endearing and persuasive. Despite my nervousness about the whole thing, I had spoken honestly and direct from my heart, because I had tried everything else on the personal beauty market and believed in these products completely.

The venture got off to a great start, but looming ahead was another tantalizing incentive that required me to push even harder. The owners of Seacret were holding a conference in Arizona the following May, six months after our spa party, with special activities planned for the top performing members of their organization. I so eagerly wanted to be part of that inner circle and continue to grow my partnership with Jason.

We were constantly on the phone with each other. We would be online together for weekly training sessions. We would even have conference calls with the owners of the company. We often teamed up to make phone calls together to prospective customers, including Jason's sister-in-law whom he was trying to recruit as an agent. Sometimes bringing in my point of view helped him: "Talk to my friend Nancy who used to spend hundreds of dollars a month on skin-care products before she started using Seacret. Now she only spends $100."

We were helping each other in this push to get to this invitation-only Arizona honor, which was reserved for top-selling Bronze, Silver, and above Seacret agents. Getting to Bronze was not easy. I had to sign up fifty customers on the monthly product replenishment program. And six of those had to become agents themselves. It forced me not only to reach out to my current network of friends, associates, and acquaintances but also to dig up my old Rolodexes to find and reconnect with people from the past.

That's why they were calling it "relationship marketing." It was definitely way out of my comfort zone. But I did it. Part of the rationale behind our approach was not to frontload our communications with shallow marketeering to just get a sale. Instead, the big idea was to connect with the person and sincerely give a crap about what was going on in their lives. And you had to mean it.

At my day job running my company, a certain degree of people skills was required. But my interactions with my employees were strictly businesslike—demanding nothing more personal than remembering birthdays, spouses' names, and the like. At work, I was a disciplinarian standing apart from my employees and the clients for whom I worked. I had to maintain a certain demeanor with them to command their respect, and I could never let my guard down. But this new exercise selling Seacret turned all that upside down and forced me to let my human side out.

Putting skin cream on the people at the spa party opened the door to get more personal; it offered an icebreaker to talk about what else was going on in our lives. It doesn't get more basic than the fact that our skin is the most noticeable thing about us, and we all should wash our faces. And all of us in a certain generation are noticing how we're getting older and more wrinkled. Everyone is concerned about the bags under their eyes. My contemporaries were chiming in, "Yeah, I'm starting to get like that too." It was surprising how that one topic fundamentally began to shift the dynamics of my interactions with many of my colleagues and business acquaintances. We got deeper into relationships and less into outcomes, deliverables, and objectives, the kinds of dull things I'd been immersed in with my "regular job." It was not my imagination that the atmosphere at work improved as a direct result.

What was bizarre, and this was something that Jason had warned me about, was how the people who were going to get involved with me were not always the ones we might expect. No one can predict in a group of thirty people at a spa party who is most likely to sign up. Just as no one could have foreseen that I would ever become friends with Jason. Or him with me!

What was also totally unexpected was how this venture provided a vehicle to open up relationships that I wouldn't have had otherwise. "What are you doing in your life?" I would ask people. "Are you happy in your job? Tell me about your friends . . ." One good example was the wife of one of my employees who came to the spa party. We were casual acquaintances at best, sharing only a passing, "Hi, how are you" at one of the office parties. But surprisingly she came up to me and said, "I've always wanted to do this type of thing!" I became her coach, and in some ways that had nothing to do with selling the products. We became very close on a personal level. She wanted to get her medical degree, and I found I could help encourage that. I also deepened my relationship with my sister-in-law after she became an agent. We replaced the usual superficialities at family gatherings with meaningful conversation. I developed a rapport with the wives of my stockbroker and accountant. It was crazy how simple it was to open up new relationships.

CHAPTER 5

Rhino Renegade

Another big payoff was about to arrive in Jason's Craig Holiday connection, which admittedly was something I didn't quite get from the beginning. The twelve-week online training taught by Craig was not an official part of the Seacret program, but it was certainly in alignment with the caring core values of the company. It was made available only for those who were under Craig Holiday's umbrella. In other words, Jason was my upline, and Craig was Jason's, so we were all part of the same network. Every time I signed up a new customer, both Craig and Jason would also benefit.

The mention of "there's going to be this training" led to the natural assumption that it would be all about skin care. That was my wrong first impression #1. My wrong first impression #2 was what a waste of time this was going to be.

Yet the Craig Holiday online training, which was mandatory for all of us on Jason's team, started off on the wrong foot with me on two fronts. A woman who was supposed to provide an overview of the basics of the business presented the first module. Unfortunately, she spoke to us very slowly and deliberately, almost like we were preschoolers. Maybe she was imparting terrific information, but it came across as patronizing and dull. Glitches with the PowerPoint presentation didn't help. "Now, we're ready for Craig Holiday," she mercifully concluded. I'm a skilled corporate speaker, and it was hard to take. Also, when he started speaking, Craig came across with a bit of a hardcore evangelical vibe talking about God and how "we are all blessed," and so on. That did make me feel a bit uncomfortable. I remember thinking to myself, *What am I getting myself into?* But if Jason believed in this so much, then I could at least keep an open mind.

I was afraid to tell Jason what I thought at first, thinking he might jump down my throat, but our conversation put my misgivings to rest. If anything, the talk we had increased our rapport. He agreed that the woman had taken some credibility away from Craig, and Jason said he would talk to him about it, which he did (and the woman soon faded into the background). In response to my discomfort over the religious part of it, Jason easily put my concerns to rest. "Well, you know, I'm half Jewish and half Mormon." So if he could deal with it, then so could I.

Once the introductory part of the course was done, Craig dove into the heart of the material. And he was an amazing motivator. He called his program "Rhino Renegade." "The rhino has been the symbol of my training for years," he explained on his website. "The rhino is strong and tenacious and doesn't back down. Rhinos run extremely fast despite their size. They can last for days without water. They are incredible to behold. They are a force to be reckoned with!"

Craig was himself a force to be reckoned with. He had trained more than 80,000 people over three decades and had thousands of subscribers in addition to Jason and me. He had made a comfortable living from it. Not too bad for a troubled, overweight child who grew up in subsidized housing—and later, a college dropout who became a construction worker. Somehow he had faith in himself that there had to be a better way. "Without money, without any worldly goods, I held on to the belief that if I could overcome the neglect and abuse that tried to push me down, I could accomplish remarkable things—and bring people with me." He was hardly a guru on a high pedestal; instead, he was someone who had worked his way up from the bottom, and who spoke with authority and empowered and inspired us through his example.

Rhino Renegade was presented as a step-by-step process to build your own business. In actuality, it dove quite a bit deeper into the internal work of tapping into the true self. The rationale was simple—if you are happier and living life more passionately on the inside, you will create more abundance, forge better relationships, and be all the more productive in your work on the outside. True, selling skin care provided a safe, pragmatic, and accessible platform to do some things I might otherwise have found every possible excuse to avoid. But I loved everything about Craig's teachings. I felt like if nothing else came out of the whole Seacret experience, the Rhino Renegade process was worth it by itself.

By applying these teachings and working hard, my efforts yielded major dividends. On Black Friday (the day after Thanksgiving), typically the busiest day of the year for retail sales, I was the #3 top producer in the company. I achieved the Bronze level. Springtime in Arizona was nearing.

CHAPTER 6

Arizona

The trip to Arizona was not just a chance to see some cacti and breathe the dry desert air. In addition to enriching the business partnering and friendship with Jason, I would get to better know the Seacret company and its founders, whom I had grown to admire, as I learned more about their enlightened way of doing business. The centerpiece to the trip was two days of dedicated training with Craig.

The very first event on my schedule, on the night before the main conference started, was a pool party at Craig Holiday's home, a good distance from my hotel and close to the middle of nowhere. And of course, seemingly to get my adrenaline up, I got lost, or so I thought. I was driving around and around an oasis-like community without luck; finally, I gave up and called Jason. "I'm here, but I don't know where the hell I am," I told him, and we both started laughing. He gave the phone to Craig, who told me I was, in fact, not lost. "You're right outside our front gate." It wasn't the first or last time he helped me find my direction.

Walking into his place and surrounded by a sea of new faces, I felt like I was back in high school. I was the new kid; although, I'm sure I wasn't the only one who felt that way. Some of the guests were in the pool, while others stood around in shorts or jeans on dry land. A few I could recognize from their photos on the Facebook group, and of course there was Jason and a couple of his people with whom I had only spoken on the phone, but I was essentially adrift among strangers.

Some of the party guests were in cliques, and others were clearly not. "Oh boy," I shuddered, realizing quickly how I had been so sheltered and protected in my marriage that I'd never really had to be socially self-reliant in this kind of setting. I couldn't even recall the last time I had to work a room and go up to strangers and ask them to tell me about themselves.

I decided the best strategy was to assume my corporate persona, because the alternative would have been freak-out mode. "If I put my work face on, I can deal with it," I assured myself. No one watching me walk into a business meeting would ever think that I had any issues with self-esteem and confidence. The businesslike "Hi, I'm Nancy" approach seemed to work out all right. Almost immediately, I had a particularly nice interaction with a friendly couple from the Midwest. We exchanged pleasantries but didn't get too far under the hood during that initial conversation. That broke the ice, and I moved on from there. *My experience as a seasoned business executive had been good for something at least*, I thought.

If I thought Craig's place was in the middle of nowhere, then the location for his workshop at a Courtyard by Marriott the next day felt positively intergalactic. It was an hour and a half drive from my hotel and, to make matters worse, I was late. GPS finally got me there. The training had started a half hour earlier at 9 a.m., and I was far enough behind schedule to completely freak out.

By nature, I start feeling physically ill even just thinking of being late for anything.

My entrance felt like one of those recurring nightmares many of us get, such as showing up at school at the wrong time for a final exam to find only an empty classroom, except that this time it was real. Here I was walking into the room of about twenty or so people. Every seat seemed to be taken. There was no easy way to slink into the back of the room. My heart was beating like thunder. *They're going to think I'm a flake*, I feared. My old patterns of behavior and thinking had grabbed a hold of me. The group had mostly elected to stay at a local hotel close to the workshop location. So they were rested, on time, and looked relaxed, while I was completely stressed out.

"Hi Nancy, there's a seat next to me," greeted Jim, the husband of the couple I had connected with the night before. "We've just taken the lunch order," said another person at the end of the row, who I had also met at the pool party. "Give me your order." They were taking care of me. I was calming down a little bit.

Then I looked at the printed agenda. It showed a list of people who were speaking. My mind began racing. What? We *all* have to tell our stories? This isn't what I signed up for. What do they mean, tell my story?

Okay, I seemed to remember from the briefing that Craig said everyone was going to do something like that. So maybe it's all about how I got into Seacret, who my upline is, and that sort of stuff. About four participants had already spoken before I got there, among them Jason, according to the list. *Oh, great!* I thought, wishing I had gotten to see my friend speak, to provide a clue to how I should talk. I was alternately panicking and trying to calm myself down, to get the drift of what was happening. To my relief, I learned that Jason actually hadn't yet spoken—they had switched him with someone else; he was going to speak later on.

I listened as Craig told his own life story, setting a high bar for the others by revealing a lot of the struggles, traumas, humiliations, and demons he had faced in his life. By exposing his own vulnerability, by telling his own foibles and failures, the guru and master was making it safe for the rest of us to dive headfirst into uncertain waters. His technique worked.

One of the first speakers told a heartrending story that boiled down to this: "When I was a little girl, my father died. Years later, I got involved with this guy, and he was abusive, and he took a gun and threatened to kill me. And he beat me up!" Oh my God, these speakers were cutting to their core! Nobody spoke about mundane stuff like how wonderful the Seacret products were, or how their new career was helping them afford a night on the town.

I scanned the list of those remaining and, with a giant sigh of relief, realized my name was not on it. I suddenly became very "chill" and sat back to just listen to others pour their hearts out. A few turns later, Jason got up to give his talk. "I thought I was coming here to talk about Seacret, but that's obviously not what it's about," he laughed, as he put his prepared notes away. He offered a nice assurance that I wasn't the only one who hadn't gotten the memo! Jason spoke about his father and his family. He didn't get as deep as some of the others and registered much lower on the wet Kleenex index, but he did open up a bit. As he finished, the announcement came that it was time to break for lunch.

Finding a place to sit in the dining room proved almost as awkward and nerve-wracking as my tardy arrival. I—the seemingly confident, high-achieving corporate executive—was suddenly transformed back into that anxious teenaged outsider clutching a tray in a lonely school cafeteria. Again, I experienced that feeling of alienation where everyone else seemed to know each other, with lots of, "Hey, Joe, what's going on?" banter in the background.

My mind flashed back to when I was eleven years old. My parents had come to rescue me from a horrible, school-sponsored camping trip after only two days of what was supposed to be a week-long stay. "Can't I just go home? I feel sick." I had pleaded with the school sponsors. My parents were contacted and agreed to pick me up after my father got home from work later that evening. The campsite was a good two-hour drive from our house, and it was not a fun ride for my parents on a weeknight. In exchange for releasing me early from the campsite, the school insisted my parents take me to see the school psychologist, a man by the name of Dr. Sigmund Pickus, a promising-sounding name for a shrink! The best he could tell them was, "If you don't deal with this issue now, you are going to have problems with her later in life."

The whole Seacret setup was also a bit odd, with people seated at tables with others they knew and darting in and out to pick up their orders. I had the last order; I just stood there with tray in hand surveying the room, flustered about where and with whom I was going to sit.

I saw Jason sitting at a table with his people. Another couple I had met the night before invited me to sit with them. But before I could sit down, Jason appeared. "Excuse me, you're with me," he said. His simple gesture of offering that empty seat beside him assuaged all my lurking childhood fears. It was a kind, simple gesture that was hardly out of the ordinary for him. But it mattered to me. I had never felt so accepted by someone I hardly knew. My isolation, my shell, suddenly dissolved. I was in Jason's group. I was part of his team. It sounds odd, but something happened to me in the company of all of these strangers that I had never allowed in my life before. I was opening up.

During the online training prior to Arizona, I sensed how Craig could be a bit of a tough guy in a tough love kind of way. "I know which one of you guys is not going to be here in a year because

I've been in this business for a long time," he told us, making me think of him as a drill sergeant during basic training. We all had to account to him, and my job was to try to make Jason look good to Craig. But along with the toughness, he promoted a spirit of healthy competition among us. When I did well on Black Friday and got kudos from him, it was incredibly validating. I realized Craig had become a sort of father figure to me. And I saw I was not alone in this. I learned that he did a lot of work with men who had difficult issues with their fathers. Hmm, another reason why I may have been drawn to him. Once I came to Arizona and met him in person, I could see how powerful he was as a communicator and motivator.

When the last speaker sat down, Craig stood up and began to wrap up the session. "And that concludes our . . . oh, there's one more person who's going to speak. She came in late, but . . ."

As I was listening to this, I knew with a sinking feeling that my free pass had suddenly expired, and I was going to have to go up and spill my guts in just seconds. It didn't help that, while all the others were giving their talks, I'd been going through my own mental exercise of thinking about what I would say if I had to. And I had come up with blanks.

I got up and walked to the front of the room, not knowing what I was going to say. What came out spontaneously at first was the story of Cassidy. That incident was still fresh in my mind because it had only happened a few months earlier and had been so powerful. I shared how prior to that turning point I'd known deep inside that I was existing in emotional lockdown. Yet I'd not been in a place to do anything at all to fix it. I described the devastating impact of my father's illness on my childhood and how his untimely death had affected my career and life choices.

Continuing, I talked about how the only way since early childhood that I could get in tune with my emotional side was through listening to music. I spoke about the Pink Floyd and Bon Jovi songs ("Comfortably Numb" and "I Just Want to Live While I'm Alive") and how I'd heard them a million times before but was now suddenly consciously awakening to their messages. I shared how I had started going to therapy to fix what was broken in my life and how I realized that I had a chance to make a personal, even spiritual, comeback. Lastly, I spoke about how through my training with Craig and my relationship with Jason I was starting to come into my own. "I don't want to just exist, to be numb. That's why I'm here and grateful for this opportunity to experience this with everybody else in the room." The essence of my remarks all boiled down to this: it was like I had been screaming my whole life and no one could hear me—until this moment. Telling them my tale was incredibly liberating; I felt like a prisoner released after many years in confinement. It all came pouring out, my whole story. Things I would never have related to anyone just a short time before.

It is hard to put into words the intensity and the dramatic release of energy in the room that afternoon. Everyone was opening up and giving voice to thoughts and feelings that had been padlocked away in the deepest recesses of their psyches. In my own case, as one of the speakers had related, no one had ever put an actual gun to my head. However, the emotional anguish of a child, even under less dramatic circumstances, can reap similarly toxic consequences, and it had for me.

The simple truth was that I had never really expressed myself to others because I didn't think anybody really cared or understood me. After too much disappointment, feeling dismissed, or misunderstood, a child gives up on trying to be heard, and that pattern of behavior can linger on through adulthood. Speaking in front of this group about my inner life involved a quantum leap of faith, ending nearly a lifetime of self-imposed silence. Until that afternoon, the only thing that anyone saw in me was a tough businesswoman. No one in my adult life had ever seen me in my actual, vulnerable state. No one ever saw me cry. People had exposed things about themselves in that room that, although greatly therapeutic, no one wanted broadcast to the rest of the world.

At the end of the session, Craig said, "We all have a bond here that will never happen again. You all will remember not only each other's names but also each other's stories." He was understating the obvious. As the long day concluded, everyone got up to leave. A couple of people came up to me and shared positive sentiments before I, too, full of thoughts and mindfulness, left for the hotel.

After quickly changing, I went downstairs to the restaurant bar and met Jim Forbes. He had flown in to videotape interviews with me for the corporate coaching series we were producing. (More of the invaluable Mr. Forbes in a later chapter.) Then Jason appeared and gave me a hug like I had never experienced. Tears were rolling down his face. "Oh my God, Nancy, your story!" I will never forget the look on Jim's face, wondering, but not in a weird way, what in the hell had taken place. In chorus, we told him, "You wouldn't believe it."

The next day, other people from the group said similar things. "Wow, your story was amazing! And you didn't know you were going to talk!" Sometimes it's best just to take the plunge, without preparation. As Craig had predicted, we hung together like a band of brothers for the rest of our time in Arizona and continued to stay in close touch long after. The actual conference itself became almost anticlimactic.

Coming back home posed its own absurd challenge. Some people around me recognized and accepted that I had returned as a different person. But most remained locked in the same head-space and stuck in the same rut. They tried to make me feel weird that I didn't want to do the same things anymore. Some could feel the shift, but my efforts at expressing to them what had happened in Arizona were hard for them to comprehend. How could they really understand? The frustration of trying to describe how I had changed was a painful reminder of the past that I was leaving behind. I didn't want to go back there ever again.

All of those strangers in Arizona had embraced and accepted me for me—for who I really am—and I wanted to keep that going. I decided to start fighting for what I knew I wanted to do, what I had to do. The whole experience gave me a confidence and a strength I didn't know I had. I was not going back to the person I had been.

This entire change in direction would make me shift from one job of "moonlighting" to another. Within a few months after returning from Arizona, I hit the pause on my second career as a skin-care salesperson. While I still loved the products and the company, it was clear it was taking up far too much of my time for the financial return. Jason realized the same thing. I decided to start spending my time figuring out how to completely change my life and be truly fulfilled. When all was said and done, Craig Holiday and Rhino Renegade was the big takeaway. Jason and I were both grateful for how much we had learned from the experience.

CHAPTER 7

Colors

It can be a scary thing to start changing everything at the same time, but just dipping my toes in the water was not an option. Going back to my old, pre-Arizona self was nonnegotiable. This new direction in my life that I call my "Second Act" mandated a headfirst dive, sink or swim. Nothing short of being all in would get any meaningful results. And it meant a lot more than just coming up with a new line of work. Breaking free of my old patterns demanded that I dig deeper and figure out how to make some serious changes to my personal life.

The middle stage of this transformation brought a whole new set of obstacles. Many of these were not the fun stuff of fulfilling my fantasies but hardcore, "How badly do you want this?" tests of will. On one side was the euphoria of reconnecting to my dormant creative self, which I had put on the shelf since dropping out of art school decades before. But my feelings were tempered by the kind of adversity that real life brings, such as juggling the responsibilities and obligations of an already busy professional and social life. But as I soon learned, underneath all of it was an even larger reclamation project.

What I had experienced with Jason, Cassidy, and David the psychologist was just a preliminary step. Opening that doorway to my locked up inner world was a monumental accomplishment. But once over the threshold, I had to clean up my toxic load of fear and repressed emotions. And I was eager to do it. Where previously I'd done everything to avoid stepping out of my emotional comfort zone, now I felt confident and excited to face my obstacles and challenges head-on.

Soon after realizing that I had come to the end of my therapy work with David, my inner voice said it was time to see Cassidy again. A year and a half had gone by since that first mind-shattering reading with her. I didn't really question why it suddenly felt right to go back. Was it simply to get a reassessment? No, I actually didn't know why, and I didn't need to have an answer. However, my intuition was clear that there was a lot more inner work to be done if I was really serious about my Bon Jovi motto: "I just want to live while I'm alive."

I don't know if Cassidy remembered me from before. She made no outward reference to our first reading. Rapidly getting down to business, she told me that she felt chakra balancing and crystal therapy would be the way to go if we wanted to work together. She then started explaining what all of that entailed. Chakra balancing is an East Indian concept about energy centers in the body that ward off disease and build emotional strength. The related idea of crystal therapy uses gems and crystals to heal ailments.

My old self would have run screaming from such esoteric notions. Previously, I would tune out and roll my eyes when people started getting overly theoretical or intellectual about things. Anything that smacked of New Age spiritualism was a nonstarter. When I was twelve years old, everyone in my family learned

Transcendental Meditation (TM), a result of my father's interest in the health benefits of meditation. My parents took me along with them to the introductory lecture, but I was not interested in the science-based studies and theories of TM so I did not start practicing with them. However, a year later I decided that I wanted to do it because of the positive changes I saw in my family. I have continued the practice to this day because of the positive impact it has had on my health, feelings, and well-being.

Had I gone online and looked up chakra balancing, I would have discovered quite a body of literature on it. But I didn't feel the need to research it because, at this point, Cassidy had credibility with me because of that first reading. New Age nonsense or the real deal, I mostly gave Cassidy the benefit of the doubt. Certainly I was ready to jump into the driver's seat and find out for myself.

Another message came in the form of a hidden master, just as I was beginning to have doubts about whether Cassidy and her practices were legitimate. Was she authentic, I began to ponder, or just looking for my dollars? Her approach was both time-consuming and expensive: Would it be worth it?

Yet hidden masters can appear at the oddest times and in the most unusual places. Such is the story of Monty . . .

On a spring afternoon in late May, I was in a local shopping mall about to meet my friend Robin for an early birthday dinner. I had arrived a little early to get her a card and to find suitable wrapping paper for the gift I had purchased for her. With my large shopping bag in hand, I was walking toward the escalator, about to go up to the next mall level to the card shop, when a man approached me. He was wearing a red tracksuit, sneakers, and a baseball cap and was carrying a black leather portfolio that looked like it held an electronic tablet or iPad. He was a light-skinned African American, tall and thin, most closely resembling the rapper and actor Ice T, who appears on one of my favorite TV shows, *Law and Order Special Victims Unit.*

"Excuse me," he said. I thought either he was going to ask me to take a survey or to join a religious cult. Ninety-nine out of one hundred times, I would have cut him off right there and said, "I don't want any." But something made me stop and look at him.

"Excuse me," he repeated. "I have a 'calling from above and a special gift.' I was sent over here with a strong message for you," he said mysteriously. "I was on my way to my spa appointment, but I was told to take a detour. The message was, 'You need to go and talk to this woman by the escalator.' I could already be in the steam room now, but a strong calling from above told me to stop and find you." He paused. "There was a huge glow emanating from you, so I knew the message was meant for you."

I should have blown it off, right? My gift needed wrapping, and I still needed a card. And here was this weirdo. But I stayed and listened.

"You are amazingly creative. There's a huge energy emanating from you. You're in a creative field, yes?" It seemed like Cassidy all over again. Still, I thought he was a flake, and I wanted to test him. So I told him, "No." But he insisted over and over again that he was right. He didn't stop there. For the next five or six minutes, he spoke in rapid-fire fashion, not stopping for me to respond.

"You are beautiful, but you obsess about your looks and your exterior beauty. You are obviously well put together, but you need to understand that your beauty radiates from the inside, and it's your love and wisdom that makes you stunningly beautiful. Stop feeling unattractive and obsessing about your looks. You are 5,000 percent more beautiful than most.

"You are about to see a huge shift in your life over the next thirty to ninety days. You will experience happiness that you can't even begin to imagine." He went on. "Your work—you are going to be making a change, and you will be very happy. You gave up your dream, but it will soon be realized in a big way.

"You needed safety in your relationships but didn't realize that it was already within you. You have a masculine energy, and you use self-control to make it appear that you are tough. But after about six months or so, you will drop your guard, and the special man in your life will say, 'Who is this? This is not what I signed up for . . .' It is when you allow others to see your softness that you become truly amazingly beautiful.

"You are a writer, an amazingly talented writer," he continued.

The mysterious stranger went on: "Your dreams are about to unfold. You lost your spontaneity. You lost yourself and checked out for a while. You deserve happiness, and it is on the horizon. The time for you is now."

While I was listening to all of this, and despite its strong and remarkable ring of truth, I was expecting him to hand me a business card or tell me, "For $500 and a visit, I'll tell you more." But that didn't happen.

He concluded, "By the way, what's your name? Mine is Monty."

"Nice meeting you," he concluded abruptly and went off to his appointment. With that, any lingering doubts about my work with Cassidy flew out the window. This experience was both bizarre and uplifting, and it was certainly no accident but a synchronicity of some sort. This happened long before I ever noticed TV shows like *Long Island Medium* in the mainstream media. My encounter with Monty was something completely out of my realm of understanding. The big lesson here was clear—important messages come when we least expect them and when we need them the most. I was starting to believe again.

In my first return session with Cassidy, she easily pierced through my protective armor. "You obviously don't know how to express your emotions and your feelings," she said. She suggested that I start keeping a daily journal, writing down exactly what I was feeling. That made sense. Right after our meeting I went straight to a local store and bought a bound notebook. The first entry was pathetic: "I woke up, went to work, and then I came home." Day two was little better: "I woke up, went to work, got frustrated, etc." But within a short while, things began to loosen up. I got a little more descriptive about what was on my mind. I went from not being able to fill a page to finishing notebook after notebook; the initial trickle of words gathered into a flood of emotions raging through my pen.

The chakra therapy began at about this time too. Cassidy explained the seven energy centers, which go from the bottom of our spine to the top of our skull and outward, and how they correspond to various emotional, physical, and spiritual attributes. When blockages and imbalances occur through our reaction to stress, trauma, toxins, and other damaging elements, they can show up on the chakra level, manifesting into all sorts of health problems from emotional disturbances to chronic disease. Chakra balancing, she assured me, could be very helpful in getting unstuck, in loosening the chains of these harmful ailments.

The therapy itself was conversational in nature. Cassidy would begin each session by checking in with me on how things were and what particular issues might be front and center with me at that moment. It was more spiritual than cerebral; although, she never used that word to describe it.

One of the other quite astonishing phenomena concerned the crystals that she gave me, which corresponded to each of the chakras. Each time we started work on a new chakra, I would be given two crystals, one to put on my nightstand and another to carry in my purse. It was an easy enough thing to do. Each week I would bring the stones with me for her to look at. Almost every gem went through the same bizarre process—transformed from vibrant colors to becoming virtually sapped of all tone. Though safely in my possession, some crystals would also develop small fissures and cracks and look like they were about to fall apart. One stone even appeared like it was rotting from the inside. I was convinced that I must have some pretty intense crap inside of me to do this to these stones! The therapy was intensive and prolonged, by the way, hardly fly-by-night: the chakra and crystal sessions took place over an eighteen-month period.

The other major homework assignment that Cassidy designed for me seemed a little strange but not freaky strange. "Nancy, I want you to wear certain colors as we work through the chakra balancing," she told me. "We're going to start with orange."

"Really, I should wear orange? What do you mean?" I recoiled a little at the thought.

"Just go and buy something orange to wear."

So I went to a high-end shop and bought an orange V-neck sweater. I soon realized that I was going about it ridiculously, spending too much money on these clothes.

In fact, Cassidy told me I didn't need to do that. And she informed me that the orange fabric would be better next to my skin. So, I went from buying expensive sweaters to looking for orange underwear at lingerie stores. Of course, I didn't want to have to wash out underwear every night, so I had to get multiples. It was still kind of expensive. Finally, I settled on getting tank tops that cost $10 each from a local department store. Before long, I had garments of every tint. They were something I could easily wear underneath my business suit jackets at work.

Cassidy realized something that I was totally oblivious to: the old me didn't have a single item of color in my wardrobe. Everything I owned was black, brown, or beige. So I was essentially going from wearing no color to the full spectrum, an apt metaphor for my life—a kind of Joseph's rainbow coat of many colors.

This explosion of hues gradually opened my eyes to a new way of doing things.

If I got stuck on one chakra for a while, then I'd be stuck wearing the same color. For weeks, I had to wear Kelly green, and I seriously didn't like that color. But strangely, I would go from feeling ridiculous in it to absolutely loving it by the time I was done and assigned a new color.

All the time I was wearing this rainbow of colors, I was also scribbling away in the journals. The emotional content became more intense, with copious underlining throughout the pages as well as picket fences of exclamation marks. Things I had never expressed and had long repressed were now pouring out. Cassidy got a good dose of all my toxicity and could understand why the stones she gave me were wearing out.

Then came the proud moment when she told me that I didn't need to journal any longer. She could finally ask me how I was feeling, and I could actually just tell her. I wasn't that robotic machine going through the motions of work and life anymore. I was a human being with real feelings and emotions, and in the process I was getting stronger to deal with all the stuff that had scared the crap out of me.

I started noticing a subtle but profound difference as I worked my way up the chakras, most noticeably in how other people were interacting with me. Their attitude was changing, especially at work. In truth, what was really going on started with me. I was clearing out a lot of my negative, poisonous, pent-up feelings, and people felt the shift in my energy. I started thinking differently, less angrily, about people who had bothered me in the past. I would look at them and think, *I don't feel that way about them anymore.* What a release, and relief, to let that negativity go.

I suddenly wasn't putting up such a protective wall, against others, but was instead coming from a place and perspective of wanting to help them. Since I'd behaved like a machine, I had also projected the same unreachable persona to others by not regarding my employees as human beings. I didn't realize I'd had such an arrogant attitude at work or that people had become scared of me.

I was gaining courage about the things I'd been afraid of, and I had a newfound confidence. More than wearing colors and smiling a lot more, I was actually happier, and the people around me could see that. An example of my new self had to do with my hair. The old me had never liked it. The new me decided to take control and get beyond my fear of change. It may not seem like a big deal to change hairdressers and try something different, but for me it was a huge step. I was feeling better about myself, whether I looked better or not! It suddenly didn't matter. I was learning, not really how to get my own way, but how to get out of my own way.

CHAPTER 8

Nothing to Wear

Reawakening the creative side in me took expression in one of my long-time passions—clothing design. Like everything else, I had shoved my interest in this area to the side for decades as I caved in to a "pragmatic" and repressive way of being. But that stifling attitude began to crack just like the crystals.

Necessity is the mother of invention as the saying goes. The issue I was facing and wanted to do something about was the fashion lament voiced by millions of frustrated women at the office around the world. Namely, "I can't find anything to wear," or more accurately, "I can't find something that I truly want to wear." This is not only about a desire to look our best—it's also about the practical matter of finding things to wear that are powerful and businesslike without sacrificing our femininity.

This sisterhood of dissatisfaction was in my face a few years back when I was one of twenty top women CEOs honored at an awards ceremony. The Brava Awards are organized on a regional basis by *Smart CEO* magazine to celebrate distinguished female business leaders. Such recognition is still consequential to support and reinforce the societal shift of having more women included in the ranks of senior managers. Only a generation ago women at the top of the corporate ladder were as scarce as lemon trees in Siberia.

As we all gathered on stage after getting our plaques, I could immediately sense that just about everyone felt the same glum way about what she was wearing. Behind the smiles for the camera, no one looked enthused about the fashion statement she was making. This may sound trivial or superficial at first glance, but stay tuned.

It was in fact worse than that. Every woman (except for me) was basically wearing a variation of the same shapeless shift dress. At least they were not all the same color! Deep down, we all had wanted to look our best for such an occasion, but we all had to make do because of corporate expectations and the lack of fashion options available. As for me, I wore a high-end designer pantsuit, which was definitely against the dress code—a bad compromise for someone with nothing good to wear and no time to deal with it.

For years, I'd been frustrated by the limited choices in stores for career wear. As women, we are often judged on our appearance in ways our male colleagues are all too lucky to avoid. This is even more challenging for women in leadership roles. We mostly get "uniform-like" options—suits and dresses in different colors and fabrics—usually in monochromatic colors—those dreadful shades of black, brown, or beige. There really isn't a lot of creativity in what we see on clothing store racks. The styles are devoid of anything remotely sexy that might put us at risk of not being taken seriously by our peers and coworkers.

"Yeah, we want to look powerful AND feminine" was the sentiment echoed around the table at a breakfast event I attended the next year with the Brava Award winners. The conversation took off when we all took turns introducing ourselves and telling a little bit about what we did. None of my tablemates seemed to care so much about my day job, but when I spilled the beans about my new design venture, it hit a nerve. I told them how my frustration about the clothing options for women in business had spurred me into action to design my own clothes.

I soon found out that these powerful women all shared the same frustration, especially about how most clothing stores offer little of anything that we actually want to buy (and it's not only about style but also about quality and distinctiveness too). On the most practical level, what passes for quality among the premier fashion brands these days is sad. The fabrics have become cheaper. Buttons fall off. Nice linings have become the rarest of commodities. Even if I happened to find something that came remotely close to my taste, I might still have to spend hundreds of dollars to have it altered and still not have what I want.

Turning this frustration into action, I took my old sketch pad from art school out of the attic and started designing my own clothes. I then took my ideas from paper to finished fabric by working with a wonderful seamstress. We would go together to the fabric store to pick out the material. As I got more experienced, the designs became more sophisticated—and the comments started coming. "Where did you get that?!" It was encouraging how many people were excited about my creative work. So, I thought, *Maybe I should do this for other people?* The old insecurities that had been in my head since art school quickly shot it down: *You're not talented enough to pull that off.* However, my confidence was beginning to build slowly because of the simple act of making things for myself and the positive reactions I got from others. Not to mention my sessions with Cassidy. What also helped prime the engine came from one of those moments where someone says something seemingly off the cuff and yet unknowingly plants a seed. To get ready for a photo shoot related to promoting my new book, a stylist was looking through my closet for some suitable outfits. Hanging there was my dad's army jacket from World War II, which I had inherited from him along with his dog tags. I treasure these things. Just for fun, on the spur of the moment, I put it on.

"Look, my dad and I are almost the same size," I told the stylist. "I can actually wear it."

"You should have it altered," the stylist suggested.

"That's a great idea," I replied, but promptly had second thoughts about it. Doing anything to alter that precious jacket felt like I was violating something. Mulling it over, I thought maybe I could make a new version of the jacket, drawing inspiration from its fine details but redesigning it into something both timeless and contemporary—and feminine. Hmm. The more I thought about it, the more the idea began to take hold.

What eventually began to emerge was a natural blending of some big inspirations and influences in my life—beginning with my college art studies, and my father's army garb, and my newfound interest in creativity—into something new and different. None of what followed was either premeditated or fully conceptualized. What I was doing on my sketch pad at home in my den, outside on the patio, or upstairs at one of my favorite perches overlooking the streets of Georgetown (at the Old Glory restaurant on M Street), was as intuitive and spontaneous as the whole episode with Jason and Seacret had been months before. Or as my sessions with Cassidy had become. In the end, the creative math of something that initially seemed so abstract added up to something that made perfect sense, once the end products were sewn and displayed on their hangers.

Since my father's military jacket was from the 1940s, it was maybe not such a huge leap that I came up with the idea to merge it with the amazing flair, style, and sensuality of women's fashions from that same era. From childhood, I loved seeing classic Hollywood movies, my favorite being *Mildred Pierce* (1945) starring Joan Crawford.

On top of that, I wanted to also blend in my interests from a later era, rock music, by featuring aspects of stage costumes I admired, such as those worn by legendary guitarist Don Felder in concert and in music videos.

The puzzle pieces of the statement I was making fit together like this: The epaulettes, brass buttons, and other functional aspects gave my creations a feeling of authority and power. The elegant contours of the 1940s suggested a subtle, classy sensuality and comfortable femininity that the Brava Awards women and I craved. And finally, the leather-trimmed collar, stylized neckline, and other details from the rock world costuming added an intangible edge. After all, most female executives would agree that there is a significant degree of theatricality and stage presence required to be successful in their jobs. The consensus that morning at the Brava Awards breakfast was that we shouldn't all be stuck wearing shapeless uniforms that make us feel bland. If we're supposed to have "made it," and can't reflect that in what we wear, then we've lost something of ourselves that's more important than fashion sense.

My table companions agreed that the standard way to express a touch of femininity is mostly restricted to the neckline—a little lace on the collar or maybe a bare hint of cleavage. Otherwise, everything is covered up as though we are nuns. Heaven forbid we should send a message through our style of clothing that we in any way climbed up the corporate ladder by demonstrating our sex appeal. In my own case, I would button up and cover any clue that I had a body underneath. I actually went so far as to have my seamstress make my clothes baggier to ensure that nothing would show.

The talk grew understandably lively, fueled by the kind of relief you feel when you finally have an opportunity to clear the air on a rarely discussed matter. And yes, women enjoy talking about their looks. This meeting was both therapeutic and reinforcing: I found

I was certainly not alone in feeling the way I did. There was an audience, a market out there for these things.

It's true that, at face value, the what-to-wear problem is not high on the list of critical global issues. But the stakes get higher when you look at the broader failure and disconnect. Take a look at the ridiculous images and impractical designs that the fashion industry promotes versus the way women actually look and dress. It shows how off track things have become.

Beyond the unattractive selection at retail stores, many women absolutely dread going clothes shopping because the dressing room mirror delivers a painful and degrading rejection. Most women's body shapes are not compatible with the sleek, idealized forms the designers prefer and promote. The "women" featured in the fashion magazines and used as fit models for designers are mostly teenagers who are made up to look like they're adults. I'm not heavy by any stretch, but there's no way I'm going to look good in the clothes promoted by the magazines. I'm not a 5-foot-10 teenager, and I'm not on an extreme diet. As a teenager, I may have had hips like those models, but rarely will you find a woman over twenty-one years old with that body shape.

When you scratch beneath the surface, you begin to understand just how underserved women are in getting what they truly want in their clothes. Most of the major designers are creating clothes to fit adolescent girls, not a real woman's body.

With very few exceptions, the industry is not listening, and it is not surprising to me that some top-name designers have gone out of business in recent years. Occasionally I find an item of clothing that I like, but it is harder to rely with any certainty on the few high-end fashion houses that I could depend on before.

In my previous book, *Work Zone Madness! Surviving and Rising Above Workplace Dysfunction*, I talked a lot about the concept of the servant leader. These are the kind of leaders who put integrity, quality, and the well-being of the communities they serve ahead of shareholders and profit—a rare breed today. It seems that many design houses have shifted their focus from their customers' needs to the bottom line, a result of corporate pressure to shave costs and maximize shareholder profits. Designers are forced to compromise the quality of their products to achieve their target cost reductions.

Many of us do the same thing on a personal level, by accepting lower standards, and buying into things we know are out of sync with our core values. We compromise our integrity. All too often we dismiss it with a shrug—"that's the way of the world these days. If I don't do it, someone else will." We're only following (society's) orders.

It's funny how hard I had to arm-wrestle that part of me that hates rubber-chicken dinners to go to the Brava Awards that day. Again, my intuition had the final say. "You need to go," it said. "Maybe you can contribute something helpful to the others." Unexpectedly, my fellow award winners did just that for me. I was learning that improvement could be continuous, as they say in business school, but it could also come from many different and unexpected directions.

CHAPTER 9

Inspiration

Once this feeling of creative spirit took hold, I didn't need to search far for sources of inspiration and motivation. With all the inner work I had done to clear out the negativity, finding that stimulation became nearly effortless for me. I was on the right path, and I was sticking to it. Back when I was mired in my old ways, I had all sorts of excuses ("too tired" and "too busy" headed that list). But it doesn't have to be that difficult. Taking care of the creative, inspiring part of our selves can become as much a natural, automatic part of our daily routine as brushing our teeth. Brushing up our soul is more like it, and we don't have to climb to the mountaintop to get there. Once we are open to it, inspiration can often be found on our doorstep.

True to my nature, my sources of inspiration proved unconventional at best. I seriously doubt anyone reading this book will share the joy and excitement I have at spending inordinate amounts of time in a neighborhood fabric store. It is almost embarrassing to admit that I can easily spend three hours or more browsing at

G Street Fabrics in Rockville, Maryland. God forbid if I'm buying buttons: it can turn into five hours. But I choose to spend my time at places of creative joy and fulfillment.

As I'll explain in more detail, my inspirational urges led me to design an entire line of military jackets and clothing. When looking at the clothes I've designed, people are surprised that the materials in my product samples were sourced from G Street and not from some chic suppliers in New York or Milan. Although I've been to many sources in the big cities, none of them get my creative juices flowing like G Street's fabric warehouse. In my mind, buying local is also the right thing to do, and the short car ride, when I need to quickly find a button or lining, sure beats the countless hours wasted traveling to distant locations.

"I get a headache every time I go in there," people complain to me, referring to the sensory overload of seeing thousands upon thousands of fabrics piled from floor to ceiling. That's not the way I feel. I see opportunity. I thrive on gazing at the sea of colors and touching the multitude of fine and not-so-fine materials. (Thank you, Cassidy, for helping me put color back in my life.) To me, it's all about finding the diamond in the rough.

From the second I walk in the door, my ritual begins; as it has hundreds of times before when I was only making clothes for myself as a pure hobby. I know exactly where to go. "Have you received anything new?" I ask one of the longtime employees.

"We've got in some great stuff in the back," might be the answer.

The salespeople there know my tastes. They share the passion I have for fine fabrics, and they go the extra mile for me. (Another great reason not to take that plane to Milan.) They also bolster my spirits with constant reminders about what they think is important and special about my approach: "Keep the quality.

Don't compromise your standards. Stay true to the vision you have." Exactly my own thoughts.

Most of the time I have a good idea of what I'm looking for. If I'm working on a trench coat, I will have already clearly sketched it out mentally and on paper.

Olive-colored fabric and red lining might be on my mind when I arrive, but sometimes my preconceptions change. The beauty is that I can draw what I can't describe in words, thanks to the invaluable lessons I picked up in art school.

I always leave room for discoveries. Perhaps I might find something better in a beautiful jewel-toned blue material and take it home with me. But whatever I choose has to fit the palette of my taste. One of my helpers there says that I have a good eye for and knowledge of color, texture, and quality. She often encourages me to take the bolt of fabric outside, because it can look very different in sunlight. When that magic moment comes and I know I've found just the right material, my excitement is palpable. By then there is no second-guessing.

Coming into G Street is also an important part of my education process. "What is this trench coat material called?" I might ask, because I'm still learning the basic terminology of fashion's components. But the salespeople there never make me feel stupid, although I can feel that way when I don't know the name of a certain stitch or some unusual pleat!

In the big picture, however, they understand that the right vocabulary is not what's important. They know that I'm serious and want to learn. I come in prepared, often with my sketches in hand. I was most surprised to find that they want to help because they're also inspired by what I am doing. I get energized having people around me who know more than I do. It's such a great way to learn, and I love to collaborate. It's easy to understand why I can spend hours upon hours there!

G Street is not the only place I go for inspiration. My other favorite destination is Georgetown, the urban village two miles west of the White House. There is an old-world elegance in the beautiful, historic buildings, mixed with a modern feeling and energy.

Restoration Hardware and Sephora, a French cosmetics store, are two of my regular Georgetown destinations, for reasons similar to my affection for G Street or the Old Glory restaurant. When I walk through their doors, the sensory feeling and inviting atmosphere feed and energize my soul, whether I'm there to buy, browse, or just sit and soak it all in. At Sephora, the subtle nuances of makeup tints on display are barely perceptible to the naked eye, yet they're highly stimulating to me.

"Why do you keep going in there to buy new eye shadow?" my closest friends have questioned.

"I love the colors," I reply.

"But it looks like the same color you bought last time," they counter.

"Actually, no, they are very different," I tell them. Although there are slight variations in hue, I have to admit that it is something of an obsession, call it a special treat, but thankfully not an expensive one.

The Ralph Lauren store in Georgetown stands out above them all. And what happened to me there one day is another improbable, humbling, and awesome manifestation of a higher, unexplainable dimension. Sometimes things happen in our everyday lives that are beyond coincidence, with serendipity and odds so astronomical that there has to be something else at play. Profound messages often come to us most unexpectedly, disguised in mundane matters, which slip through our resistance and help us face certain truths we have masterfully avoided for ages.

On face value, what happened to me there was not hair raising at all: you be the judge. I went into the Ralph Lauren store when I was early in the color therapy process with Cassidy. This was still a new thing for me, a big departure from my monochromatic wardrobe, but one I suddenly and openheartedly embraced nonetheless. She had told me I needed to stay with the color orange for a while. I decided to try Ralph Lauren for some new options. The store was located in one of the most distinctive and beautiful historic buildings on the main street.

Once inside the store, I immediately scanned the clothing racks, honing in on anything orange. In the back, against the far wall, I could see an orange plaid shirt—and it was the only thing there in the right color. Unbelievably, like Cinderella's glass slipper, it happened to be my size, and it fit me perfectly. A bonus: it was on sale!

Then it hit me. Incredibly, this was the same kind of orange plaid shirt I had been wearing the last time I saw my father alive. I did a mental double take. Yes, my old shirt was indeed a Ralph Lauren, and yes, it was orange, and yes, it was plaid. Orange was my father's favorite color. "You really cheered me up," he had told me in the hospital awaiting surgery, pointing to the color. We cried. Next came my remarkable epiphany—that final moment with my father had been the last time I can remember wearing anything with color.

When I tried the shirt on, I suddenly felt my father's presence in the store. I heard him saying to me, "It's time. You need to move on."

I started to get very emotional right there in the store. The sales manager and the salesperson were right there with me, incredibly understanding, as if they knew, too, that something remarkable was taking place. My connection to this place and to the two souls sharing this experience with me was beyond profound. A short time afterward, I returned to the store. "I have this amazing feeling here," I shared with the manager. "I know, I can tell," she replied. "You can come here after work if you'd like, later in the evening." She asked, "What is your favorite soft drink? We'll have it for you next time."

When I returned, I realized that my father's spirit or whatever I had experienced was no longer in the room, as if he had only lingered there just long enough to give me the message. Remarkably, the manager and salesperson, seemingly like guardian angels, had moved on to other stores and positions without a trace soon thereafter.

Once I started cracking through my stifling shell, my world kept expanding. I found discovery and inspiration in the smallest details, even around my home, that I had been too preoccupied to notice. Sitting out in the garden or in my upstairs study with my sketch pad and charcoals literally set the table for tapping into my creative side. Using such media is somewhat unusual. However, when I need to modify or re-create a drawing, rather than starting from scratch, I can trace over the old one. If I were going to do this full-time and had the luxury and more importantly the time, maybe I would try harder to make perfect, beautiful drawings. But I just didn't have the time. While it may take five minutes to do the initial sketch, modifying it to perfect the design takes a lot more effort.

Inspiration comes to me in many different ways. It may come from seeing something really striking or edgy in a catalog or magazine. It can also come from an item in my own wardrobe with a small feature I like. My father's old army jacket from World War II that I cherish so much had opened up another rich doorway to creativity. To develop this further, I got a coffee table book illustrated with military designs throughout the ages. The volume is chock full of great ideas. I also keep front and center a stylebook of

1940s women's fashions, and photographs of my favorite rock music legends in their stage costumes. I can draw on all such sources of inspiration, which are always at the ready. These diverse fragments of inspiration are some of the ingredients I use to develop my own distinctive styles.

New ideas seem to come out of nowhere when we nurture our creative self. Who knows, perhaps in a month or a year from now, all of these books, stacks of magazines, and clothing samples I have out on the table right now will have served their purpose and be replaced by a completely different collection.

It's hard to leave the subject of creativity and inspiration without discussing Transcendental Meditation (TM). I know from my own forty-plus years of regular practice, validated by numerous scientific studies, that TM unleashes the power of your mind in ways that maximize its performance and capacity. One of the many benefits I have seen for myself is that TM helps the coordination or coherence of the "left" and "right" sides of the brain. Put simply, the left side deals with the logical and analytical part of our minds, and the right side has to do with the spatial and artistic sides. TM has enabled me to better handle stress and to switch emotional gears. Balancing both sides of the brain lets me be inspired, creative, AND practical, which is a huge asset for an entrepreneur and designer—someone who's both prosaic and poetic.

CHAPTER 10

The Camera Doesn't Lie

Jim Forbes, who was there with me in Arizona gathering footage for a *Lunch and Learn* series (more on this later), is one of those hidden masters who appeared in my life at the right time to put jet engines on my wings. Jim is a fourth-generation journalist, writer, producer, and distinctive voice talent, best known for his VH1 series *Behind the Music*.

The seed of my keen interest in documenting things on film that ultimately brought me to Jim comes from my passion about my family history. Over the years, my relatives have entrusted me with a great number of photos and artifacts for safekeeping, from scrapbooks to home movies. I love having this archive because I'm sentimental at heart, and each one of these relics has a story to tell. They document the many ways big and small by which we leave an indelible mark on others during our lives. A notable and unlikely example of a most prized possession in the collection is the plastic onion my beloved Aunt Harriet had in her kitchen. It conjures up all the joyful times I spent with her.

The accountant side of me also appreciates archiving things on film, because I enjoy how the data we accumulate both documents and reveals the truth. I'm a detail person: I love the minutia. At work, I can sit with an auditor and take information down to the lowest level, and then take it back to the top-floor view, and take pride and wonder in how it all ties together, or doesn't. Similarly, with video, the history of your past events is all there in each and every frame. The auditor in this case is you and your observations. Maybe someone doesn't believe what I've been telling them, for instance about how crazy and inspiring it was when Jason did my spa party and put skin-care products on my friends. But because it was all recorded on video, I have the proof.

Some people don't like to look at images of themselves on film. But whether looking at old footage of videos or reading words from diaries or newspaper clippings from months or years past, I am never uncomfortable, even if the material is not flattering. I have become an anti-narcissist in that regard. My overriding thought is always, *Look how far I've come.*

Keeping a running account both in words and on film about the process of creating my Second Act goes back again to my intention to help and inspire others. Namely, to work through what's holding them back from creating greater joy, fulfillment, and purpose in their lives. None of this would be believable or useful to anybody if it were all a glossy, one-dimensional fairy-tale of Nancy the accountant who became the fashion designer. None of this is going to be helpful if I am not forthcoming about disappointments and setbacks. Yet showing the whole truth is not as hard as you might think.

A discarded concept put on the far back burner, or a venture that others might regard as a failure, has almost always yielded incredibly valuable information and wisdom for future success. (And sometimes has led to better opportunities and outcomes than

I could have imagined.) Being on a journey means that we are constantly making adjustments to what lies ahead. It is why the notion of course correction resonates so much with me. As Jason so often said, "Course correction is not failure." I couldn't agree more. Course corrections are a pragmatic move back in the right direction. They're a means to an end.

Five years ago, I had looked Jim up to see if he would help me with a special surprise for my employees for an upcoming annual holiday party. I love rock documentaries, and his VH1 series *Behind the Music* was a favorite of mine and of millions of other music fans. I had in my mind a vision to do a little documentary film for the party, *Behind the Parties*, a takeoff on the VH1 series. I wanted it to be authentic right down to the smallest touches, and I wasn't going to do it unless Jim Forbes agreed to narrate it. To my delight, he accepted.

As we spoke during the recording session from opposite coasts (Jim in a sound booth in Los Angeles, and me in Washington, DC), I was already thinking ahead to future business. *I'm not walking out of here until he agrees to do my next project*, my intuition demanded. So, at the end of the reading, we started chatting. I have always been fairly wise about ways to get people on board and excited about what I'm doing—enough, I hoped, to make Jim want to do what I had in mind. I brought up to him the idea of making a film on Transcendental Meditation as a company benefit and how it can improve the workplace environment. The idea was to tell the story from the perspective of my employees who had recently started practicing TM.

"Oh, I know all about TM," he said to my pleasant surprise. "I did a news story once in Fairfield, Iowa." Jim was referencing the Maharishi University of Management, (MUM) located in Fairfield, Iowa. MUM was founded in 1971 by Maharishi Mahesh Yogi. The college features a "consciousness-based education" system that includes the practice of the Transcendental Meditation technique. It was clear that Jim was not a meditator, that is, a practitioner of TM, and that he didn't he have any affiliation with the TM organization. Logic dictated that I could have easily gone to a filmmaker like David Lynch, a devout TM practitioner, and someone I know, and asked him to do it. But deep inside I preferred someone who was going to be the devil's advocate—and Jim's considerable talent for skepticism, fueled by his sense of journalistic ethics, remains at the core of the enormous value he brings to any project.

The film of the holiday party was a great success, and I was fully intending to call Jim to get the TM film going when the bottom fell out of my life. The cascade of ill fortune began when I got a call at the party that my sister-in-law had broken her foot. Things plunged downward from there. About two days later, my beloved dog Smokey died very suddenly. Hours later, my brother was rushed to the hospital for emergency open-heart surgery. And before I could catch my breath, my favorite Aunt Harriet (owner of the plastic onion) passed away. I was devastated.

With my brother moving in with us for a month to recuperate post-surgery in the dead of a winter filled with ice and snow, I, too, found myself frozen. I simply wasn't ready to take on anything new or to talk to Jim or anyone else about outside projects.

"I didn't think you were going to call," Jim told me when I finally reached out to him in March, over two months later. I told him how my world had fallen apart. "I kind of figured that," he replied. "You were so excited about the project when we last spoke."

We talked for two hours, and we immediately reconnected on a lot of different levels. In the end, he agreed to come and meet all the parties involved in the TM project as a first step. "If I do this, it's going to be warts and all," he insisted. "That's why I want you," I replied. "I want it to be real. You can have carte blanche, open access with my family and employees. You can talk to them about anything. I won't edit out anything that's unflattering."

Before he arrived, I underscored the ground rules for my family and employees. "I want you to tell the truth. I don't want you to gloss over anything. This is not going to reflect on your employment or our relationship. I'm not going to stand there in the room and listen." After he came and pre-interviewed everyone (including my mother and brother), he saw that everything was consistent with what I had pledged. He agreed to do the project, which was the first of many others.

Meditation as an employee benefit was a new idea at the time, one that has thankfully grown in popularity since the video, "Meditation Makeover: Incense and Beads Not Required" (http://www.gsfweb.org), came out in 2010. The TM organization embraced the project wholeheartedly and made sure it was disseminated throughout their worldwide network. Many of the employees featured in the film were far from the New Age stereotypes about TM. And those seemingly most unlikely to embrace it ended up having the most dramatic transformation because of it.

Before long, Jim and I were doing a lot of filming together. We went from one thing to the next, creating a library of material both for immediate use or to be stored away for the future. In the downtime between filming and editing, he was proving to be a great sounding board for my own pursuits. "No one cares about the backstory until they care about the headline," he would always say, challenging me to stay on focus.

One good example of our collaboration was a series of short videos called *Lunch and Learn*, a kind of online training for people in business that they could easily view during their lunch hour. It tackled some of the common problems almost every business faces, showing me going into various workplaces and collaborating with the owner, managers, and employees to resolve real-life challenges.

We thought seriously about making a nationally distributed TV series about it. However, the idea had to be put on the back burner; but again, it led unexpectedly to the opening of a much bigger doorway.

Hours upon hours of professional videotaping can be expensive, which was something that made Jim constantly moan in disapproval. As a journalist, he was used to working on deadline and getting projects done and finished, the story wrapped up in a tight, short package. Instead, my mind was constantly going to all of these crazy places. He would sign on to do a video about X, and by the time it was almost done, I had moved over here to Y. I was driving him insane, and he'd get really aggravated with me, but something other than the fees I was paying him was keeping him involved.

I tend to be sun, moon, and stars, with a bit of sizzle mixed in. Jim is nuts and bolts: "Let's get the facts." He listens and finds both the cracks and, more importantly, the hidden gems. By venturing into that craziness of mine, we got to some innovative areas that made him stretch the boundaries of what he thought possible with his own work. He had other talents that weren't being tapped— and being part of my "alternate universe" has helped him venture outside his box.

"You have no idea what our conversation last night sparked," I have found myself repeating over and over to him.

"I don't think I'm bringing you any value," he often shot back.

"You don't understand the value you're bringing to me," I replied.

"And you don't understand your own resourcefulness." I got him to see that he was more than just a journalist and the guy who does videos.

"I thought my job was to kind of wrangle with you, to help you synthesize all the disparate things you're interested in," Jim told me recently. "I always say, let's find your nugget, the core, and from that all things will grow. Anybody who knows me kind of laughs that I'm telling you that. They say, 'You? You're all over the place. Wow, then this Nancy character must really be out there!'"

CHAPTER 11

Convergence

When you're onto a good thing, the universe gives you a little pat of encouragement. The message can be simple and clear as a bell or cryptic and crazy in the delivery. At the core, I had been acutely tuned in even as a small child to where my passions and talents lay. I could sit for hours sketching out fashion ideas in crayons on paper, showing the drawings to my mother for her review. To our astonishment, sometimes a detail in what I drew might magically appear months later in the fashion magazines, like the winged sleeve that became the rage of the early 1970s.

I attribute a lot of my fashion sense to my mother, who has an excellent eye for style and color. When I was a child, she would often take me on shopping trips with her, which was a special treat that always lifted my spirits. Going on these trips and watching my mother select outfits for us had a strong influence on my own sense of style and love of fashion.

For reasons both big and small, this interest faded, a casualty of the cumulative weight of an emotionally difficult childhood and young adulthood, my father's death being the worst blow of all. In its aftermath, I was left having to fill in for him and take on many of his roles and responsibilities within the family. Even before, when my father's health had started to decline, I'd had to get grown-up jobs. I had attended art school, but I had no illusions about becoming self-supporting in that field. I held a number of short-term jobs where that background proved useful, such as working in print advertising for a department store, but this training was not an obvious asset for someone building a career in accounting.

Reconnecting decades later with my creative side was unquestionably a direct result of all the work I'd done with Cassidy, Jason, Jim, and the others who accelerated my inner growth and helped put me back on track. It's now clear that the seemingly random, accidental, and divergent stream of events led me to my inevitable destination.

Regarding those more cryptic messages from the universe, the biggest catalyst for making such radical career and life changes took the form of some extra-stressful drama. It was as if the gods were testing my resolve as I moved closer and closer to the big shift. It is like they were Jewish mothers admonishing us, "So if it was this easy, then everyone would be doing it."

The next stage was set while I was working with Jim Forbes, in a final push to get the *Lunch and Learn* web series off the ground. Several episodes were already in the can, including one about a well-established but rather worn restaurant that needed some serious upgrading to attract a younger generation of clientele. I still wanted to do one last video about working with a fashion designer.

Toward that end, I had identified a wonderful, young New York designer whose work I admired. "She really gets it," I said to myself. So I went to New York to meet with her, and our relationship developed from there. She understood how I could possibly help her from a business perspective and agreed to be filmed for our series. The next big challenge was getting the upscale retailer she was featured in to agree to let me film her trunk show in its store. Amazingly, they said yes. They told me how they believed in what I was trying to do. Everything had fallen into place, and Jim and his crew were all booked.

Coming down to the wire, the designer called me and dropped a big bomb on the whole project. "I'm sorry, I can't do it. You can't film me and you can't interview me, because I'm doing my own documentary now, and I'm not allowed to have others film anything else about me."

Canceling filming was not an option for several reasons, and there was no way I'd flake out on Jim, who was already running short of patience. I had to come up with something quick, and Jim came through as usual as a valuable sounding board on our plan B. The idea was to find another designer and use an upscale shop in Georgetown, named Giotto, as the location for a trunk show. Nicky, the boutique's owner who has known me as a customer for years had agreed to host the show: "Whatever you need," he told me. "Come down and do it." Our next problem was finding a designer in less than one week. Good luck!

The only option to save the shoot was to feature a so-called designer I knew very well—me! Yikes! Jim proposed the idea that I should stage my own trunk show, with my own designs. I was there to help other companies, after all. But now I was suddenly throwing the spotlight on myself—an ironic twist, and absolutely the furthest thing from my mind. We were also stretching artistic license to the max.

I hadn't really planned to ever do anything with the jackets or any of the other clothes I had made, other than wearing them myself. All I had in hand were two jackets I had designed for myself—the military jacket inspired by my father's uniform and another, edgier one with a rock star/military-style flair inspired by an exhibit, a time capsule of Bon Jovi's stage costumes over the years.

Organizing this show in such a tight time frame would mean that we would have to scramble to film the elements of putting the clothing together, from sourcing the custom-made buttons and fine materials, traveling to the fabric store, and working with the seamstress to create the finished product. Remarkably, everyone consented, with the exception of the seamstress, who was not comfortable being filmed. Esther, an employee at the fabric store and a sewing virtuoso, agreed to stand in for her. The pieces were coming together in a rush, and everything was staged in almost the polar opposite of what we had planned just a week earlier. The filming became the engine driving everything else. My subject bailing out on me created a domino effect that pushed me to do some things that I felt very uncomfortable about and that I would have never done under normal circumstances. That's the kind of effect that I usually have on Jim, but this time he was having that effect on me.

We filmed the show, and I breathed a sigh of relief—we had made it work and salvaged the video shoot!

However, something else was brewing on the West Coast, inside Jim Forbes's fertile mind. When he got back to Los Angeles and looked at the footage, Jim called me, ecstatic. "You know, I think Nicky was serious. He really liked your stuff. I think you ought to talk to him." I countered that the store only carried high-end Italian designers, the very highest-end. They operated in a world that had nothing to do with me. I did these jackets for myself, just trying to find a route to express my creativity. Any idea of making a business out of it was unimaginable. But I listened to Jim's advice. I went back to Nicky's shop, again carrying in my two jackets. "What do you think about what I'm doing," I asked him.

"I think it's fantastic," he told me, looking directly into my eyes. "I'd love to do it with you." He would feature my clothes in his store. When I had recovered from the shock, Nicky proceeded to give me a road map of what I needed to do, down to the number of units and the range of sizes I needed to supply his store, and pricing as well. I would deliver four different styles and came up with the label name of Tseneh (tSEEnah), the Hebrew name bestowed on me by my parents and, coincidentally, a term that can mean "departure" or "arrival."

Things were falling into place. It would be hard to find a more ideal place in which to test-market the line than Nicky's Giotto. I could make all my mistakes on a small scale with a dear friend before attempting to take it to a higher level. Suddenly, Jim wasn't angry with me anymore for wasting my money and his time. Instead, he was truly stoked and gushed over my work like I had never heard before.

"I'm starting to sound like a fashionista," he laughed. The puzzle that we were attempting to solve suddenly fit together with effortless ease. All the Craig Holiday Rhino Renegade stuff was bearing fruit, showing what can happen when the full force of your passion and natural gifts start to emerge. I put another lesson from Craig to good use: developing relationships with the enthusiastic people who were supplying my clothing materials. Manufacturers of specialized leather and customized buttons took pains to help, even though my orders were not the most lucrative. They just seemed happy to participate in my own joy themselves. Cassidy and Monty's predictions were starting to take hold. All of my business acumen and my artistic aspirations joyously came together in wonderful symmetry to guide this project.

Anthony, my jewelry designer friend, was there with tough love, spurring me on by berating me: "You're not a real designer. This is not the way to do it!" That criticism made me dig in even more against the trappings and conventions of his world. My rebuttal to him was simple: I have never done anything the way everybody else does—that's why I'm in the 1 percent of self-made people. Do you think Bill Gates or Steve Jobs stayed inside the box? People like them—who have broken out big time—typically hated school, felt constrained doing what society expected, and thought differently than other people did. My mind doesn't work in a normal manner. But when you see the finished product, you see my madness has method.

It was as if I had come full circle. I was finally pursuing something I'd had buried within me for a long time. "It may or may not work," I told myself, bracing for possible failure. But as with everything else, I was ready to dive in headfirst with unbridled enthusiasm. The little girl still inside me was jumping up and down and couldn't wait to get her colored pencils out again! And I was now ready to leverage all the business skills I had gained to make my own venture work.

CHAPTER 12

Reality Check

My jackets were designed, sewn, and placed on the racks at Nicky's upscale boutique, its Georgetown locale the best of possible test markets. Encouraging signs were coming from many directions: customers were saying, "We want to see more." Clearly it was time to build on the excitement, ramp up, create more designs, and expand my products to showcase my range and ability; and quickly, in time for the fall buying season.

But earlier that spring, the universe had something in mind other than my best-laid plans. Things would soon come to a grinding halt. It was enough to give me an ulcer, or shake my newfound faith. It is tempting to lump all of what I'm doing as though I'm in the middle of my own reality show on television. Many of those programs show people chasing wealth and fame through glamorous pursuits. In fact, Jim and I worked on a pilot for a reality show of our own. Like those shows, this book gives you the front passenger seat for a ride on a journey without a predetermined destination. But the comparison of my life to a reality show ends because my challenges cannot be nicely tied up, resolved, and packaged into thirty-minute, easily digested chunks. And no actors are needed to create artificial conflicts to keep the action and intrigue going.

If the situation were more like a manipulated TV program, then people might assume that my life was more like a cakewalk. "Look at her, she's got everything, she has it made." "Hey, if I had some money to invest, I could live my dreams too." If that were the case, then all the pieces would fall effortlessly into place, right? Sounds easy.

However, this isn't reality TV. I don't have unlimited funds. Everything doesn't always work out the way I expect or want. Reality checks can take many different forms, and some that have happened to me are too complex for television, or they aren't exciting enough.

One of my goals in writing this is to tell the real story and not gloss over the truth. Authenticity means showing defects, as well as triumphs, and not a pretty fairy tale that is of no use to anyone. While I may have more financial freedom than most people, when you peel back the layers, there is not that big of a difference between the average person and me. The toll of my day job—being a CEO and being responsible for more than twenty employees, the stress of maintaining top-notch performance at all times, and the long hours put in before I can have fun doing my design work—can hold me back significantly.

Sometimes, manifesting the initial, euphoric success is the easy part of the journey. Trying to take it to the next level releases a whole new set of challenges. It can be a grueling, gut-wrenching test of grit and will. Be prepared to strap on your helmet and get ready to stave off the setbacks, make course corrections, and most importantly never give up. I'll do whatever I must to stay in the game. Whatever endgame goal I have in my head is only a placeholder, and for good reason. Setbacks are inevitable, and the opposite is also true. Experience has taught me to stay open to the possibility of even greater opportunities ahead than I may be realizing at present. That way of thinking is especially valuable during those times when it seems that all the wheels are about to fall off. Which is exactly what happened as I was about to ramp up production levels on my clothing line.

I had to push the pause button and put everything on hold because the reoccurring, five-year federal contract for the day job I had held for the past seventeen years—the work that was funding my new business ventures—came up for renewal. To keep this work, I had to face a grueling trial by fire, one that I had been through painfully many times before during contract renewal. Not only was my livelihood at stake but also the livelihoods of dozens of my employees as well. Several other companies would be bidding against us, to try to knock us out of our contract. And while over the years we had done an outstanding job, which was very clear to our customer, the outcome of any government procurement process is very unpredictable.

Keeping this contract was crucial to my Second Act plan. Some might ask, "Why don't you quit your job and just go for it?" In fact, I'm sure if you questioned people who have embarked on second careers, the majority of them cleaned out their desks and made a clean break. I could have done the same thing, but it was not the choice I ultimately decided to make. I had my reasons.

At the core, I intrinsically do what feels right for my circumstances and what I'm trying to achieve. The day I'm not happy with this approach, then I'll go to a different model. For better or for worse, I'm not willing to jump off the train into the unknown. The practical business side of me says, "You've got to slow down, even if it may take you five years to get there. You don't want to go in too deep because you want to make your mistakes on a smaller scale." That's why working with Nicky at Giotto appealed to me.

I told myself: "Don't put yourself all in, and get backers forcing you forward, and start spending money that you may never get back." Keeping the income flow from my other job meant the freedom to maintain control both creatively and business-wise. Outside investment could come in later once the venture was on solid ground.

I also believed my story had more credibility if I kept my day job. Consider the difference between the headlines: CEO MOONLIGHTS TO LAUNCH SUCCESSFUL CLOTHING LABEL versus CEO QUITS HER JOB AND IS STRUGGLING TO GET BY.

One of the biggest stress points in this sudden crisis was that there would be no advance warning of the announcement date and deadline for the new contract proposal. Everyone knew the notice was coming, but we had no idea whether it would be this week, next month, or three months away. Once the government published the notice, we would have very little time to prepare our proposal. The tight deadline would put us into crisis mode, which would move my clothing designs to a low priority. Forget about planning a vacation or even a weekend getaway.

Think about competitive athletes who have their personal routines for psyching themselves up to get ready for the big game. The sprinter knows the date and time for her race well in advance. Likewise, the starting pitcher knows the next turn he's going to get and prepares accordingly. My problem was we never knew the game time. We didn't have the luxury of knowing in advance the timing of the notice, or what the work would be, and thus what would be required for our proposal. Further, my employees were nervous about being in limbo. I knew everyone was wondering, *When's this going to happen? Will I still have a job when the process is completed?* I felt helpless and powerless, which was the reverse of the surge of optimism and creativity I had been experiencing.

After months of waiting, the request for proposal, or RFP, finally came out on a Thursday, in the form of a seventy-five-page document mandating, in excruciatingly fine print, what would be required for a winning proposal. Details such as font point size and margins, page counts, and other minutia were clearly laid out in the RFP document. This would be the third time in three years we had received this "call to action," because the government's two previous attempts had been canceled at the last minute due to its own errors. We were glad to see the basis of the contract award decision criteria had not changed from the last two; namely, demonstrated technical skills, management ability, and past performance would be significantly more important than cost.

In short, the award would be based on "best value"—whether the contractor could successfully perform the work at the contractor's quoted price. For this reason, and because our government customer valued our work products, we felt confident that we could win the contract. However, we knew the proposal would be a lot of work, and we would have to be very careful to address every point and adhere to the strict formatting requirements.

Overlooking any one of these small details could result in having the entire proposal thrown in the shredder—along with our jobs. Lack of painstaking attention to detail was not an option for us. Even a small slipup in formatting could make our proposal invalid and make us ineligible for award. And we would have to sharpen our pencil a bit—look at cutting costs, to make sure we remained competitive. Of course, the government has a reputation for surprises, so we couldn't afford to be overconfident. Still, our feeling was something akin to "cautiously optimistic."

Of course, this was all happening at one of the busiest times of the year, including at the government's own fiscal year-end. My personal machine would have to find a new gear and go into overdrive to cope with an already all-consuming schedule, from being the nucleus of all our business operations, overseeing every part of our government contract, as well as managing all the internal affairs of our company. Add into the mix the responsibilities of personal life—cleaning, shopping, cooking, taking care of the dog, and helping out my family. Exercise, maintaining a healthy diet—anything to take care of myself—was also put on hold. My Tseneh design activities went into lockdown until we completed the proposal.

After a long day of work at the office, I finally got to scan the seventy-five pages of instructions for the first time. I immediately went into "I am overwhelmed and panicked" mode. The enormity and painstaking tedium of the task hit me. My pity party would go on for the next twenty-four hours, which is the maximum I allow myself for letting go of all the emotions and then getting myself back on track. As you might be able to tell, I'd much rather have been designing jackets.

Along with the crush of this new burden, I reflected on how this would be our third proposal over the past three years. The government had already made two attempts to award a new contract for the services we had been very ably providing for more than a dozen years. It seemed unjust, frankly, because we had saved the agency literally tens of millions of dollars. The disappointment resulting from each of those attempts had barely healed. The whole experience provides an extraordinary view into the often-illogical inner workings of government, which is much too large a topic to detail here.

My husband and fellow top executive Rick and I knew we could put together a terrific proposal when we put our minds to it. But it wasn't like we could just recycle all the data from the past go-rounds, because the agency constantly changed the rules of the game. However, at least this time it was more flexible in giving us more time to do the proposal as well as granting up to sixty pages for our response. (One of the previous RFPs had allowed only ten double-spaced pages for our entire response to a fifteen-page single-spaced task description!) At least we wouldn't be pulling all-nighters as we'd done previously. Still, we would have to use every available hour after normal work hours and before bedtime, and all our weekends and, if necessary, take days off from our busy workday schedule to make sure we followed each instruction and answered each question. We needed to convince the decision makers reviewing the proposal that we remained the "best value" to the government.

Once my pity party was over, I had to find the drive to deal once again with the proposal process. That effort requires a huge amount of discipline, determination, and energy. You know you'll be giving up your life during a big block of time, so get that coffeepot ready because you're going to need it. I actually had to buy a new coffeemaker because my caffeine consumption wore out the one I had. As usual, Rick and I each found something inside—a personal resolve—that said, "I can do it! I won't let this get me down. I'm going to do it!"

Four weeks later, the proposal was turned in. Rick and I felt we had pulled out all the stops; we were at peace that we had done everything in our power to successfully roll that boulder up the hill. Now, the matter was out of our control.

There was only one problem in the aftermath. Me. Not taking care of myself and working like a dog, an over-caffeinated dog with a broken coffeepot, and without the release and lift of my new endeavors and newly rediscovered talents, had left me with an ulcer. The burning pain that resulted was so great that I couldn't swallow my own spit, let alone anything else. I was like one of Cassidy's cracked stones. But I still had to go to work. There were things that had piled up, people's problems to listen to, and urgent matters to attend to. I had to sit through meetings while struggling to speak. It would get so bad that at times I couldn't breathe. *I think I'm going to be sick,* I thought to myself while in one of those meetings. I excused myself, walked down the hall to the restroom, and then went back to my desk to finish my appointed tasks.

Health destroyed, frustration at a crazy level, and feeling like the weight of the world was on my shoulders—it was easy to understand why I couldn't at first get back my artistic design mojo. The machine was broken, shut down. After turning in the proposal, it wasn't as easy as flicking a switch to get all the moving parts of the design venture back on track. I had to do something to get myself out of this funk, I told myself after a week of feeling awful. *Enough! Take action. Go to Georgetown, a place that inspires you. You're never going to get out of this until you start moving toward a different alternative, a better alternative.* So I took my sketch pad and went to my regular table at Old Glory. At first, I still looked and felt like someone in the ER ward, but in the end it was the perfect medicine.

Once I had gotten back in balance, I discovered a big silver lining in the midst of all of this upheaval. I experienced another transformation, about my regular work. No longer did I look down on a day job that kept me away from what I loved. The pain and suffering had taught me that the work was there for good reason—and this made me realize that I had to earn that contract back because I had taken it for granted. Of course, I had wanted to keep it the other two times we created our proposals, but this third time was the big wake-up call. This time I really wanted it. Gratitude and appreciation for all the remarkable opportunities my job afforded me had replaced all my negative emotions.

It would be several weeks before we would learn the outcome. But I was completely at peace. The transition from my beloved design work back to the reality of the grind had been jarring, and I'd suffered because of it. But I felt better. And my mojo was back and even stronger.

CHAPTER 13

Worst Fears

"Oh my God, oh my God, I can't believe it, I can't believe it," I repeated for minutes in total stunned freak-out mode. Buried in the email I was reading was news that struck like an exploding grenade, its shards piercing though my carefully reconstructed world. Call it the fulfillment of one of my worst fears. We had lost the contract!

My heart was pounding out of my chest, and my whole body was shaking in shock, disbelief, and anger. At least I wasn't crying. Maybe it would have been normal for other people to cry in this situation, but not for me. I guess I don't react the way normal people do—a fact that would prove a surprising strength as things kept unraveling.

On September 28, a Monday evening after work, I decided to check my office email as is my habit. Sent to both Rick and me, and to a number of key employees on my team, was a thread of memos back and forth between the government officials responsible for selecting the winning proposal. Sifting through the bureaucratic jargon and acronyms, I quickly discovered that this email was most definitely not intended for our eyes. Someone had screwed up big-time by distributing it to us.

The email tipped off the recipients that the new five-year contract for which we had bid, and that we had every reason to believe we would win, was in the process of being awarded to another company. The memo admonished the intended readers not to share this information with me or anyone else in my company until the formalities of the decision were finalized and official notice given.

And as if the situation was not already stressful enough, our existing contract was set to expire within forty-eight hours. Our contract had many complex loose ends that would force us to make some rather important endgame decisions under sickening duress.

I immediately got on the phone with Rick and, telling him to open his email, said, "You're not going to believe this!" The memo had also gone to four members of our staff, which put us into full-crisis mode. The staffers probably wouldn't see this until the morning, but then the news would surely spread to all our other employees like a rapidly mutating disease. We had more than twenty employees and their families depending on this contract. Like a mother lion, my first thoughts went to protecting them and looking out for their best interests. Because we picked only topflight talent, they all had considerable value in the labor market in terms of skill and decades-long experience. So finding other jobs would hopefully not be too challenging in the long term. What worried me more was their short-term well-being, especially since the extremely short notice had caught Rick and me totally off guard and ridiculously unprepared.

The first order of business was to call Beth, one of the main federal players in the contract process—and our direct manager and in charge of daily operations—on the email chain. Rick had her home phone number and made the call as I listened on the line.

"Beth, we just got this email, and some of our employees got it too, saying that we didn't win the contract. We need to know what's going on."

Beth's shock and upset demeanor on the other end of the line was heartfelt and sincere enough to assure us where she stood on the matter. Although she obviously already knew of this news, as shown in the memo trail, the final decision had clearly not been hers—far from it. Our work had made her life easier, and the change that this would represent meant chaos and sleepless nights down the way for her. The best Beth could do was tell us that she needed to make some calls. An hour later, she got back to us.

"I'm so sorry. I'm not allowed to talk to you about this right now."

Finally, we got a return call from Bryan the contract officer in charge of the decision. "I'm so sorry it happened this way—this is not the way we do business here," he told Rick. Except this time, at least, it was.

"Has a decision been made?" Rick responded.

"No, the decision hasn't been made yet. There will be an award made, and there will be a transition. It's in legal review; that's all I can tell you."

We knew all too well that waiting for legal to bless it was only a rubber-stamp formality. The conversation ended with the vague promise, "I expect to get an answer for you soon."

By 9:25 p.m. that night, we received the official notification confirming the obvious in cold bureaucratese: "Though your firm was rated technically higher, the selected offeror was also determined to be qualified to perform the requirement without any risk and significant weaknesses to the government at a competitive price that was determined to be fair and reasonable."

Since our contract ended on September 30th at midnight, the government also indicated it would extend our contract for ninety days to provide for a transition to the new contractor. At least we would have time to try to tie up the loose ends.

It would take up the rest of this book to fully describe the utter ridiculousness of the situation. The document we received that evening rationalizing the decision was full of holes. Supposedly, the new contract was awarded on the basis of "best value" to the government. Best value is supposed to be evaluated on a combination of technical approach, management approach, past performance, and cost. The decision makers concluded that this new vendor was "technically acceptable" and, when combined with the lowest cost, was the best value.

Unfortunately, those making the decision were not familiar with the complexity of the work performed or the productivity required of the working teams. And they ignored our seventeen years of successful performance on the job. Consider the difference between someone with thirty years of direct experience versus someone hired off the street with perhaps five years of related work. The cost comparison showed no consideration for the value of such efficiencies and time-saving expertise. It also showed no consideration for the current staff's direct knowledge of the complex business environment.

The report stated that our biggest weakness was the government's vulnerability if our key people left for other jobs. The report also listed the many key financial and computer systems my firm had created for the contract, concluding: "This remains a potential risk to the Government if the intellectual property has not transitioned to the Government and there is significant turnover." This statement was particularly ridiculous. We had historically low employee turnover and had fully documented the systems and processes so that they could be transitioned to the government at any time.

However, no amount of documentation could capture all the knowledge and experience of our employees, many of whom had been with me for more than ten years. By awarding the contract at such a low price, the government was guaranteeing the loss of key employees, including Rick and me. It was obvious to us that this decision was going to cause our customer some significant problems as the new contractor took over.

In the big picture, our work was a very small but essential piece in one aspect of federal government operations. We had put in place many checks and balances and internal controls to improve fiscal integrity and responsibility and to save a lot of money for the taxpayer. We had accomplished this by fighting hard turf battles for seventeen long years through multiple administrations and against many political factions. This time, however, the contracting office had the last word: its decision was final.

Our contract expired on September 30—two days after we learned about the award. Because the contract was being awarded so late in the process; as noted, our work actually required an extension to provide time to put the new contract in place and to prepare for the transition to the new company.

Our legal team is from the best government contracting law firm in Washington. As soon as we received the official notice, we contacted our attorneys and scrambled to give them all the documents they needed to help us respond appropriately—before our current contract ended at midnight on the 30th. In discussions with our lawyers that night, we realized that we could not contest the decision for a brief extension of our current contract. Its language required that we stay on an additional ninety days for a transition period to aid the new company if we lost the contract.

You can imagine the pain of having to go to work the next morning and face your employees with the shocking news that we had lost the contract. Many of our employees had been with us for ten years or longer and were like family members to us. Suddenly they would have to deal with an unknown company and management team. Everyone was going to be freaking out, but I had to be the calm leader. I couldn't be falling apart, although I really wanted to do just that. Under normal circumstances with government contracting, such a decision would have only been made final a full ninety days prior to the contract expiration, not hours before! The whole affair could not have been planned to be more stressful and unfair.

In the heat of the moment, all sorts of thoughts swirled in my head. "I'm going to bury them over this unjust decision! We're walking out! I want to nail them! I'm going to the Department's Inspector General over this!" I was disappointed and angry beyond measure. On the other hand, I had been there for seventeen years, well beyond the average life expectancy of a government contractor. Did I want to see it all fall apart? Certainly not.

There are all sorts of horror stories about armed security escorting losing companies out of the building after letting their anger erupt into some kind of unprofessional—or even violent—behavior. However, instead of a scorched-earth approach, I intuitively took the higher ground. I decided no matter what to act in the most professional manner possible. My thoughts in this regard were about making sure my employees would not suffer. "They're going to be hurt by this anyway. What can I do to lessen the pain of their loss and the difficulty of their transition?" Everyone saw how I immediately focused on the employees, which was clearly the exception and not the norm, and I believe they appreciated me for it. It was the right thing to do, the only way to cope.

For us, there was only one possible recourse for fighting back, and it would be a very expensive one, both financially and emotionally. Our lawyers advised us that we had firm grounds to mount a protest, which would in effect freeze the process in place for up to three months while our case was considered. The decision to protest would have to be made very quickly: the window to file a grievance was only ten days and, once missed, the opportunity would be lost forever. There were many factors to ponder here too. I went back and forth like a pendulum, "Should we do it or should we not?" I wanted to be vindicated in some way, so I gave the okay for the first step in that process, the creation of the legal paperwork that would be required to lay out our case point by point. However, it would cost upward of $20,000 to draft the protest, and more than ten times that if we actually went through with it.

There were other reality checks. Only about 10 percent of all protests actually win. Did I have $200,000 or more to spend or waste? And what was to prevent the agency from starting the whole contracting and bidding mess all over again six months later down the line? And possibly select someone else again, after yet another round of blood and turmoil. We might win the battle but lose the war.

I needed to make a decision by Friday, October 9. On Thursday night, I was still in the mode of "I don't know, should I or shouldn't I?" In addition to the countless hours with the attorneys, I also brought Cassidy into the process. She had switched from helping me with my own personal issues to my business concerns. This may seem odd, but I never had anybody to go to in this regard. In my business everyone depends on me to tell them what to do. But when I don't know what to do, the entire operation could be damaged or grind to a halt. Who was I supposed to go to when I was stuck? And Cassidy had shown unusually good judgment before.

Now, as usual, she was invaluable in helping me face my own demons and deep-seated worries in all of it. "Is that what you really want to do?" she asked. "Are you sure Rick really wants this contract for another five years? Do you?" I loved how Cassidy got into my face. It was clear that I had been the racehorse that had been penned in for too long, going around and around in circles. I was starting to go crazy.

All of this was sapping my energy and sabotaging my health. To make matters even worse, while this was happening, I noticed what appeared to be a few mosquito bites on my back, which turned out in reality to be the shingles! That can be a debilitating disorder. "That was one hungry mosquito," Cassidy gasped when she looked at it. I'm trying to mentally hold myself together, and physically I'm literally itching and oozing from the seams. Horrible!

When I asked Rick the big question, he did not hesitate. He was completely fine with moving on to newer challenges. I was greatly relieved; I had come to realize I felt the same way. I slept on it one more night, deadline night. When I woke up Friday morning, I knew for sure. It was so clear, so obvious. "I've got to let it go." I had been so worried about making the wrong decision and so conflicted, but now I was certain. Holding the never-to-be-sent protest document in my hands, my mind clamored, *You have the documented evidence, an independent review, not just Nancy's sour grapes. You want justice, right? You know what? Let it play out without us. Let them see what happens now. Let them bring in the new company and see how it works without all our expertise.*

You sometimes have to close one door before another one opens. My biggest fear, of actually losing a hard-won, long-term work opportunity where we'd done a terrific job, had actually happened. But once the shock was over, I found out that it was actually going to improve my life. I had been hanging on to something I should not have been hanging on to. The universe had to do the dirty work for me because I wasn't going to let go on my own.

Confronting this inner truth, I was now relieved of a huge burden of responsibility. My talented employees, I was certain, were going to come out fine. True pros, they would engage in careful planning and diligence to find new opportunities. I still had overhead and expenses and the need to generate new income to worry about, but Rick and I had no lack of confidence that we would find another situation—and certainly a much better one.

The winds of change, especially after such a long time on the same job, are never light and breezy. Things were insane all around us, and there would be three months of chaotic transition work ahead. But if I was really serious about my Second Act, there was suddenly nothing left to stand in my way.

CHAPTER 14

Image War

One of the unforeseen benefits of the storm that came crashing down around my day job was that those changes exposed the deep fissures in my persona. Really, I couldn't have come up with a wilder but more apt metaphor than breaking out with the shingles during that horribly stressful time. My perfectly maintained, protective outer shell was literally cracking from within.

Trudging to work over the prior few years, I had been most afraid of revealing any chink in my armor, given the battles I was waging. Now, visualizing success, I told myself: "I'm a general leading my troops, and I'm not going to let the shingles hold me down." I never wanted the enemy to see me sweat. With the rash across my back swelling and oozing, I became more vigilant and determined than ever before.

Except for Rick, no one had to find out about it, including my employees. I came into work every day, not missing a single beat. I didn't go to a doctor; instead, I treated myself with over-the-counter medicines.

In fact, the shingles were just the tip of the iceberg of all the things I was trying to hide, so that everyone would think I was perfectly fine. Yet during the whole proposal-writing period and its bloody aftermath, I became aware that I could no longer be in denial about how things were taking their toll on me. My employees knew things were far from perfect in the stress-filled pressure cooker where we worked. And it wasn't really helping anybody that I was trying to hide things, for example, like how I had bandaged my back to keep my wounds (sores) from seeping, literally. That was going too far. I had shielded them from so many of the past years' battles.

I never told them about all the turf wars and petty intrigues; I kept it all close to my vest. Yet again, this happy-face subterfuge to hide every weakness wasn't helping anyone. Especially me. My body was telling me, "You're not invincible. The truth—the reality of the situation—is going to come out." Maybe my role of mother lion protecting her cubs was actually not serving my employees well. Maybe they really needed to know just how crazy the situation had been. They would then have a better understanding of how much I really cared and that being the boss is not a cakewalk, sitting in a corner office and collecting a bigger paycheck.

Further, banishing my femininity to be perceived as a strong leader in the workplace went much deeper than wearing pants instead of skirts. You also had to behave like a male and hide any display of emotion or feelings. Putting a collar on emotions often means that in the process we diminish our emotional intelligence, a resource that is one of the most valuable attributes of female energy, a resource that is a big plus for both men and women. My awareness about reclaiming this part of my life had obviously been growing for some time, notably in my passion for clothing design. But the looming end of my contractual work removed the last remaining layers of my carefully crafted veneer, peeling the onion right down to its core.

I took old scrapbooks out of their dusty storage, and they were filled with poignant messages, as if they had been waiting for the right time to share their truths with me. I love reliving family history in this way. In so many photos from the 1960s, I was wearing the frilly dresses from my mother that were the fashion standard of the time. As a younger adult in the 80s and 90s, the pictures show me heading out to a concert or a night on the town wearing clothing that was equally feminine. Flash to the turn of the new millennium, and something changed. Just as the colors and luster of the old photos and videos began to fade and turn grainy, I too became progressively more monochromatic. From head to toe, I dissolved into drab suits. At first, I was clad in skirts, but soon pants replaced those. My tops were equally non-expressive—a long-sleeved shirt buttoned up to the neck, with a brooch or pin going across to secure the collar: buttoned-down Washington fashion at its most typical and uncreative, anything to mask the individual soul and to celebrate the collective.

In more recent times, when I became aware of how this important part of my life had shriveled to near extinction, the pendulum had swung temporarily to the opposite extreme. My after-work wardrobe became more vixen-like. Reflecting my love of edgy musicians, I dolled up like a rock star in leather, corsets, and pushup bras, with bold makeup to match. Cassidy, to her credit, made me realize that I was demonstrating yet another masculine trait in dressing so provocatively, aiming to get the wrong kind of attention. She helped me understand that this was not a good solution.

Resurrecting the expression of my femininity, while casting aside my hard-earned role of battled-hardened executive, has felt as difficult as giving up a hardcore addiction. Yet with Cassidy's encouragement, I forced myself to buy contemporary versions of the dresses I used to wear as a more carefree young adult. But still they remained unworn, hanging in my closet. I made excuses. "Tomorrow, I'll wear one of them, even if I just wear it around the house." On a more positive note, this inner struggle fed inspiration to my design table, where I worked to incorporate the contemporary with the classic. I struggled to find a renewed comfort and joy, with style and dignity, in being authentically female.

My ordeal with the shingles made this loss of my femininity, with my exterior appearance, my physical ailments, and with my internal psyche, even more intolerable. As stated, a big part of it was trying to stay strong, to remain this perfectly oiled machine, a fairly masculine image in itself. With the loss of the contract, however, this submerging of my femininity, like the shingles, could no longer be ignored. I realized that it was going to come out one way or another. Why not embrace it?

Reflecting on my self-image back in early youth reminded me of how many years I had been deeply unhappy with my personal appearance. I had gone through grueling dental procedures to fix my teeth from the time I was eight years old until age forty. I had always hated my baby-fine hair. I sheared off my waist-length hair when I was sixteen and was never happy with it after that. It seemed I was always on a fruitless quest for the perfect hairdresser and haircut. So I finally did something about it—and got hair extensions. Now I would finally have the long, feminine hair I had always wanted. Nothing was going to hold me back: my new journey would address the external as well as the internal.

Sharing this sort of private information publicly is part of my cure, not solely for the intention of helping others. My conversations with Cassidy revealed this innocently enough, when she asked me one day what I liked to do for fun. I told her how I loved to read.

"What kinds of books do you like to read—science fiction or romance novels?"

"No," I told her. "I love biographies of people I admire or find interesting." I went on to describe *Storms: My Life with Lindsey Buckingham and Fleetwood Mac* that I had recently read about the musician Lindsey Buckingham from the group Fleetwood Mac. You know, the guy doing those amazing guitar solos in inspirational hits like "Go Your Own Way" and "Don't Stop Thinking About Tomorrow." His former girlfriend, Carol Ann Harris, had written the book, and she went into great detail about all the challenges and difficulties he had faced, from personal relationships to health issues like epilepsy. A master guitarist, saddled with a neurological disorder, like Beethoven going deaf! Reading about his problems and how he battled made me truly admire him much more than just reading about his great accomplishments ever could.

"You need to start doing that yourself; you need to get serious about it," Cassidy urged. "Dig deep, let it out. You have to be more real, not just in your writing but also with the people around you. Show them a little bit more of what you're going through. You need to get further under the hood."

CHAPTER 15

The Graceful Exit

As the shock and horror of losing out on the contract started wearing off, I went into action mode to deal with reality. Change is never easy, and to say that the daily and weekly grind until our contractual commitments were fulfilled tested my patience and self-control is a gross understatement. I had spent a good portion of my life at that office; and despite the unfairness and utter ridiculousness of the situation, I didn't want to destroy my team's legacy of accomplishment and hard work. We were leaving the place in far better shape than we'd found it—and we wanted to keep it that way.

My ultimate decision to take the high road, as challenging and painful as it would prove to be, set off a chain of consequences that I could not have choreographed better. Believing that right action is its own reward, our steps at that time would again give me a peek at a glowing silver lining. The situation provided one of the most unpredictable and remarkable hairpin turns in my journey of transformation—and without a doubt the most decisive one.

My acting contrary to the norm caught everyone at work off guard. First, the assumption that I was going to lodge an official protest was pretty much a given in their minds. They thought, *Why create more work for ourselves by working on a transition to another company if everything goes into the deep freeze for three months because of a protest?* So, when I affirmed in no uncertain terms that we would be gone in ninety days as our contract mandated, it set off panicky shockwaves in all those people involved in overseeing the transition.

Keeping a professional and cooperative demeanor throughout adversity required patience, gritted teeth, and even some deep breathing exercises. Yet what gave me the fortitude to endure, more than anything else, was the expensive document I kept in my brief-case, the missive that would never be sent to its addressee. The letter of protest I had paid my attorneys over $20,000 to prepare was the best investment I ever made. It laid out step-by-step how egregiously flawed the decision-making process had been in award-ing the contract to the other company. It wasn't just my opinion, one that could have been easily dismissed as sour grapes. Instead, it served as a kind of nuclear deterrent, giving me the power of choice: to use that weapon in my briefcase or to move on and refuse to play a game where there were no winners. I felt a great power in knowing we were in the right. That document gave me back my confidence and self-respect.

The absurdly fine line in this transition period between humil-iation and satisfaction in a job well done was on full display in one particular episode, which epitomized the benefit of letting go of the negative to attract the new, more powerful and positive possibilities into our lives. Rick and I were finally called to the first face-to-face meeting in the wake of the big upheaval. The vibe in that room would be incredibly tense. Those running it would be prepared for the possibility of us, the ousted contractors, behaving badly and perhaps wailing and gnashing our teeth. They'd keep their fingers on the button ready to call security to escort any unruly parties out of the building. As I noted earlier, many people in my situation had reacted to such meetings like wounded bears, lashing out at their tormentors.

The email invitation from the agency's contract office read something like, "We're having a meeting on Tuesday morning from 11 a.m.–12 p.m. and 1 p.m.–2 p.m. Be prepared to bring your transition-out plan, etc." Rick's name was misspelled, and the jumbled syntax seemed like something a kindergartener had written. Adding to our discomfort: the information we needed from the agency's contracting office to respond intelligently to its request was being withheld despite our numerous requests. The game of delay they had orchestrated down to the final hour in awarding the new contract was now playing out again. It was like being forced to watch a bad horror film—one where we unfortunately happened to have a starring role.

On the morning of the meeting, we found out to our dismay that the new company management team would also be in attendance, along with our agency program representatives and agency contract office staff! "Why are they coming to *our* meeting?" I wondered. The new company had already had a private meeting with the agency's contracting officer, so wouldn't it have been appropriate for us, the long-term contractor, to have the same? Of course it would have. But we sucked it up and prepared our transition plan, despite having no information from the other side about the new company.

Rick and I walked over together and arrived a few minutes early for the meeting. Rick, a lean and handsome man, was in his power garb, a dark, smart-looking suit. Likewise, I wore a tailored brown pantsuit (and an orange top under my jacket), with hair and makeup put together perfectly. We looked wonderfully businesslike on the outside, masking the best way we could how uncomfortable we were on the inside. If I'd had my crystals with me, they would have been cracked. Moments before we started, we saw Beth, the government technical representative who manages our day-to-day contract activities, in the office suite adjacent to the big conference room where we would be meeting. "Thanks so much for coming," she said.

"Did we have any choice?" I countered with gallows humor.

"You could have called in sick," she replied.

"That would just be postponing the inevitable," I replied, and we had a little laugh.

The meeting could not have been orchestrated to be more awkward. We had not yet met the managers for the new company. Beth and her colleagues had not met them either, because the agency's contracting office, who oversees the contract award process and who ensures contract terms are being met, had prevented them from communicating directly. What's more, the contracting officer, who had called the meeting, was late, resulting in fifteen minutes of torturously uncomfortable small talk and forced smiles between contractors old and new!

Since we didn't know anyone, we suggested that we all introduce ourselves. More forced smiles.

Finally, Beth's supervisor got up and said, "I think I need to go find out where the contract officer's people are." A few minutes later Bryan (our government contracting officer and the decision maker on the contract) his supervisor, and two of his employees came in. We repeated the ritual of going around the table for introductions. Awkward! "We want to talk about the transition," Bryan began. "We'd like to talk about your plan."

"If I don't know what you're coming in with," I countered, "how can I transition out? We've been asking you for the statement of work and for a schedule on the transition."

"Well, we're working on it."

Bryan's supervisor turned to me and suddenly interjected, "We're still hoping you'll stay until the end of January."

While our contract required us to provide a ninety-day transition, the government had asked us to stay on an additional month because the transition had started late.

"Every email and conversation," I said very forcefully but politely, "that we've had states we're clearly not entertaining staying on through January. We're done on December 31st, as our contract states, and our plan lays out how we are going to get there."

Since we hadn't been given any information about the new company's planned transition, this was intended as a starting point only, a draft to get the ball rolling.

"We'd like to have you go through your plan with us," Bryan replied.

Without knowing anything about the new contractor, I read verbatim the three pages that Rick and I had prepared, emphasizing that it was just a draft. "We have no idea what the other company's plan is and what you're planning to do," I warned.

"Well, we wanted your plan."

The conversation kept going around in circles like this. I went along, even though the whole thing was ridiculous. It was obvious the new company's management hadn't created its draft transition plan; although, all the entities participating in this contracting process were required to have one. To add insult to injury, the agency's contract office was in effect asking me to lead the meeting. I was the wounded party, the head of the ousted firm, and they were asking ME how I was going to manage the transition! The total lack of decorum and preparedness on their side, plus the entreaties to stay on longer seemed to suggest they had counted on me lodging the protest, which would have delayed the transition.

By the time I got back to my office, emails had gone out from the new company to all my already freaked-out employees, stating that the new company's management team was intending to interview all of them the next day with the intent of possibly bringing them on board immediately!

Keep in mind that we had just met for the first time with this firm and that many of my employees had been with us for more than a decade. They had been walking on eggshells for weeks about their future work prospects. This was very painful for me to see—it was almost like I was told that I was an unfit mother and they were taking all my children and putting them in foster homes. Even worse, they were then asking me to stay on and sit in the front row to watch it all happen.

It was becoming increasingly clear to all parties that the whole matter was turning into a real mess. The government contract office didn't expect that I would hold firm about leaving at the end of the term of my contract after already surprising them by not lodging the protest. I was equally firm in keeping professional and respectful during the awkward transition process.

I tried to make it very clear that, in addition to not staying beyond the contract period, I wanted to ensure that my employees' occupational future would not be hurt, or at least try to protect them if I could. The government's technical representative wanted to keep them on, so I did try to find some solutions. However, it was painfully obvious from the new company's offers that many would be forced to leave. Beth and her colleagues realized the looming nightmare that would result if all of these incredibly competent people eventually found other jobs, and they would be stuck with far less experienced staff with the new company.

On a personal level, the unexpected truth that emerged was how this debacle was turning out to be a deliverance, a blessing in disguise. As far back as a decade ago, Rick and I had started talking about exit strategies, but the reality was I was only doing lip service. "We're going to sell the company!" we'd claimed. But that's not an easy thing to do, and it was especially hard because I didn't want to be the bad guy with my employees or hear them say: "Nancy is selling her baby and cashing out, and dumping us with the new owners."

How things change. When I first started working in that job years earlier, I was doing something I really liked. I was a business consultant telling my clients what needed to be done and advising them about their strategies. And at first, they listened. But because the organizational infrastructure was such a mess, I couldn't get anything further done. In response, I had to take over the chief responsibility to make things right, which took a long time. I set up the systems and practices to put their operations in excellent working order and brought in experienced people to perform the highly complex work. I became the program manager, responsible for the day-to-day operations. Getting my hands dirty with the daily operations was not something I relished, but I did it (and did it well) because I had to. All of this frustration, aggravation, and drudgery I'd suffered through at my day job made my sideline creative endeavors all the more spiritually rewarding to me.

My fears about potentially losing status and credibility as a "failed" CEO, which might thwart my efforts in launching new ventures, proved equally groundless. Because I took the high road and worked constructively and professionally with my government clients, I kept my integrity and deepened our relationship of respect as we moved through the final days of the transition. Relieved of a tremendous burden (and one for years that I had chosen not to acknowledge), new and more fulfilling opportunities were finally able to flourish.

CHAPTER 16

Park City

Keeping my dignity under the humiliating circumstances had exacted a heavy toll on my mind and health. I had already endured a torturous and horrendous ninety days of the contractual obligation to transition our work to the new company. Everyone involved in the transition quickly realized that it was not going well—in the black-and-white world of accounting, errors can't be easily dismissed or swept under the rug. The transition was messy. Small mistakes build momentum over time and grow into nightmares at year-end closing. All I could do was make sure that I held up my end of the bargain—by helping my former employees and leaving everything in good order while maintaining my reputation.

Apart from personal pride and the placement of some employees in new positions, those first three months of transitioning the work to the new company felt degrading. I was training a village of new people who didn't understand the complexity or magnitude of the work at hand. While it was now obvious that the perceived savings would likely be offset by a rough transition period and a degradation of financial accuracy due to the loss of experience, the contract decision had been made and could not be undone. Beth, our government technical representative knew this but was powerless to do anything about it. It was frustrating and sad for all of us. I eventually relented and decided to stay on for an additional four weeks beyond the expiration of the contract. My purpose: helping my employees get an extra month of income and gain more time for their own transitions.

In the waning days, my intuition sent me the strongest message to do something that made absolutely no sense—take a vacation. And an over-the-top expensive one at that, for someone who was soon to be without a paycheck! But like they say, "Go big or go home." The thought was not so much a desire to escape as a cleansing of the palate, to break the old patterns, recharge the batteries, and gear myself up for whatever was coming next. I planned to go away for five days and return for one final day at the job.

The initial spark came when I learned that my friend Anthony was going to the Sundance Film Festival in Park City, Utah, to promote his jewelry designs. Park City, like Georgetown, is one of my happy places, although at the time it had been four decades since my last visit.

When I was last there, I had been a mixed up, eighteen-year-old kid who had just dropped out of art school. I had wanted to have fun and party. Any notion that I would grow up and become CEO of a multimillion-dollar business consulting firm was totally foreign and unlikely to me then. My younger self was also not the type to win any employee-of-the-month awards either. Just before arriving in Park City, I had left a short-lived stint working for an ophthalmologist friend, a job where I videotaped cataract surgeries and ineptly answered phones. The best thing about the job was that I got to learn about the fascinating world of eye operations and even wear a white lab coat.

One day, I came in and announced that I was "going on vacation."

"What do you mean you're 'going on vacation'?" the incredulous office manager gasped.

It was classic. Here I was, a recent hire, a friend of the boss, and a terrible employee to boot. It was one of those terminations by mutual agreement.

My "vacation" destination had been Park City, where I'd gotten a job waiting tables at the Red Banjo, a pizza and subs restaurant. I wasn't cut out for that profession either—I had a real knack for messing up orders but was well liked enough to get decent tips. As I booked my trip some forty years later, I didn't think much about things coming full circle, but I wondered if the pizza joint was still in existence.

Making travel plans for Park City at the last minute during the prime Sundance Film Festival weeklong event was beyond crazy. Hotel rooms would be almost impossible to find and offered at highly inflated prices. However, I managed to book a room at a basic, no-frills, family style resort about an hour's commute from town. But as it got closer to my departure date, major blizzard warnings were looming at home in DC. Would I even be able to fly out? I scrambled to see if I could rebook my flight to leave a day earlier than I'd previously planned.

When I went online to see if I could also change my hotel reservation, a wonderful surprise popped up on the screen—an available room at one of the luxury hotels in Park City, right in the middle of all the action. Someone must have canceled at the last minute. "Hurry, last room remaining, book now!" I immediately called Rick and told him how much it was. The cost was so outrageous, beyond the beyond. But an added benefit was that the suite was so large that Anthony could stay there too, saving him the long commute to his events in Park City. And sharing the experience

115

with him would make the trip even more fun—it was getting better and better.

"I'm not going to do anybody any good if I'm in a depressed state," I had told Rick as I was contemplating whether to go to Park City or not. People had been beating me down the past three months, berating me about how my company's contract was too expensive and how they needed to get rid of me.

"Absolutely, do it!" Rick enthused. "Click on it! You need to go, and I'm insisting you do it. And I want you to go first class on the plane." Rick knew what I had been through and, as my business and life partner, his go-ahead was very important to me. My employees also chimed in. As a farewell gift of sorts, they gave me a cashier's check for $800 (and another for Rick too). Making the presentation on behalf of the group, one of them said, "We want you to know how much we appreciate you." Suddenly, going to bat for them had paid off, pricelessly.

When I pulled up to the St. Regis hotel in my rented Jeep Cherokee, it was in the dark after an hour's drive from the airport. I ended up coming in the back way, a bit lost as I'd been in Arizona. The front desk person directed me to my "butler," who would be available twenty-four hours a day.

"You have been upgraded to a very special suite," he told me.

"I bet you say that to everyone," I retorted half-jokingly, cranky and tired from the long journey.

"No, this is very unique to the property," he assured me.

I stepped into what was not a suite but a multimillion-dollar condominium that was the most luxurious place I had ever seen. Impeccably decorated and equipped down to the finest details, it was like a dream of heaven. Anthony arrived soon after—and was equally impressed! Finally, exhausted from the trip I quickly unpacked and got into bed for an amazing night's sleep.

When I woke up the next morning, I opened the curtains to a breathtaking panoramic view of the snow-covered Rocky Mountains, where skiers in the distance were gliding down the slopes. Where I'd landed was a perfect refuge of unmatched wintry beauty. I understood why Rick was so adamant that I book this place despite the great expense.

I couldn't go to Sundance without exploring all possible avenues to advance my projects. It was after all a place where film-makers came to get exposure, funding, and distribution. And I did have the fashion documentary already in progress with Jim. I had hurried to put together a business card with the working title of my new project and with an eye-catching graphic design. I knew from experience that first impressions mattered, and the more interesting the card, the less chance it would be ignored and discarded. I didn't want to look or sound like just a flakey artist with no chance of succeeding at a place like Sundance, so I tried out my spiel with the concierge and the "butler" at the St. Regis. They both seemed excited about my project, which made me feel more confident.

With almost everyone I spoke to, the conversation went: "I'm here as an independent filmmaker. I've already submitted a film here (namely the short film on meditation I had done a few years back with Jim), and my latest one will be submitted next year."

"Really? That's great. What's it about?"

"I'm doing a documentary and a book about what happens when we try to reinvent ourselves, at work and spiritually, and the film has been following that process over the past four years." And the conversation would continue from there. Everyone I spoke to expressed interest in what I was doing and encouraged me to continue on my path.

The first morning in Park City immediately delivered on the promise of being good medicine for my depleted spirits. Like a sun-starved tourist who can't wait to get to the beach, after break-fast I boarded the five-minute hotel shuttle to Main Street. It was freezing, but I spent the first few hours getting reacquainted with the town, walking up and down the thoroughfare, enjoying the icy-cold but fresh air, and ducking into shops here and there to warm up and to browse.

The place had changed considerably in the four decades since my last visit but still retained its charm. The shops that I loved the most were the ones, as in Georgetown, that you could tell had been there for a long time. My favorite was Burns Cowboy Shop, with its leatherwork and wonderful craftsmanship. Talking with the shop owners about what they did and admiring the quality of their wares was far more interesting to me than getting into the film festival stuff. Seeing the unique and high-quality "Made in the USA" merchandise was inspiring and so in sync with what I wanted to do with Tseneh.

I repeated the same ritual on the second morning after break-fast. I got in a shuttle bus with a nice couple from New York, and we talked long enough to exchange business cards. "Maybe we can help you market your film when it's ready," they told me before we got to their destination. I couldn't have orchestrated this "chance" meeting any better.

I decided to get out at their stop too because it was a part of Main Street I hadn't seen the day before. And lo and behold, there it was right in front of me—the Red Banjo! The sign above the door read PARK CITY'S OLDEST RESTAURANT. I could hardly con-tain my excitement. It was opening in an hour, but I would kill the time. Anthony texted me he was available for lunch, so we quickly agreed to meet there.

To my delight, nothing had changed. The place looked and smelled the same as before with its basic menu of pizza and subs. And the "quality" of the service was the same! With gratitude and relief, I realized almost immediately that I was certainly not the only inept waitress in the history of the Red Banjo. Having funky service was perhaps their longstanding MO; employing young people with a friendly neighborhood vibe was evidently more important than delivering the right meals to the right table. I joked with Anthony, "I guess I wasn't that bad after all."

For whatever reason, the joy of sitting there at the Red Banjo had already justified my trip. This particular day fell on the twenty-eighth anniversary of my father's death, which made it extra special. It had always been a day that I had spent in grief and seclusion, with my head buried in the sand. But this day gave me a chance to make a big departure from my usual behavior, because it was the first time that I had done something nice for myself or even remotely fun on that anniversary.

I had also brought a scented candle with me to light in memory of my father. The candle burned out precisely at the stroke of midnight that night. At that moment, I felt he was there, cheering me on, urging me to let go, just as I had felt his presence months earlier at the Ralph Lauren store.

Another important shot in the arm came from attending a party that same evening at the home of a friend of a friend who was well connected in the film industry. It was snowing heavily with poor visibility and, due to an address error on the invitation, Anthony and I got lost—leaving me feeling freaked out about being late and walking into a room of strangers—just like that time at Craig Holiday's house in Arizona. I navigated the wintery walkway, feeling grateful for Anthony's arm and the alpine boots I had bought on Main Street the day before. I knocked on the door fully expecting an uncomfortably stuffy Hollywood industry party full of people I didn't know. It was anything but.

John, the friend of the friend, introduced himself. "There's food over there; just introduce yourself to people." Everyone was so casual in almost a beatnik kind of way. Anthony hadn't eaten the whole day and immediately went over to the untouched food table. Right away, Anthony was making friends and holding court, so he didn't need me. I was ready to walk around and find someone to talk to myself.

I spotted this guy who reminded me of a young Peter Cetera (the former lead singer for the group Chicago), a cross between a rocker and a surfer dude with dark sandy blond hair. He looked really approachable. "Hi, I'm Nancy," I said. He introduced himself as one of the musicians who would be performing at the party. "There's a guy with us who used to be with the Doobie Brothers," he shared with me.

"This is my kind of place," I told him. I felt totally in my element. A couple of other musicians soon joined our circle, and we had one of those stimulating conversations about "nothing," like something out of a *Seinfeld* episode.

One of the rocker/surfer dude's friends came up to join our circle, a beatnik-looking woman with a free spirit vibe, and she introduced herself. "Hi, I'm Lisa, where are you from? I have this thing I do with words," she told me, motioning to a cloth bag she had of wooden tiles engraved with short affirmations. "Why don't you pick two of them out?" I read the pieces I fished out of her bag. "No dream is too big," read the first one. The second one just had "Self-confidence" printed on it. Not bad. That opened up the conversation. I shared what I was doing in my life and a little about my projects.

She said that she too had jumped out of the rat race. She now lived in Park City, and she was hosting the Women in Film group at her home. I explained to her that I had looked up all the events at Sundance, and the only one that I really wanted to attend was Women in Film, but it happened to be sold out.

Another woman, named Jennifer, soon joined us, and it turned out that she was one of the leaders of Women in Film. As a result of that chance meeting, a ticket to the event magically appeared. Just before the event started the next day, Lisa texted me that she had saved a seat for me in the second row with all the insiders—not bad either. Being around these powerful women in the media and hearing how they faced down gender-related issues in Hollywood was inspiring and empowering. I felt like I was in the right place with the right people. My connection with Jennifer and Lisa was life affirming and, again, just what the doctor ordered. I would have loved to hang out with them more, but unfortunately I had to leave early the next morning.

The last and perhaps most valuable takeaway from my brief vacation came from poking my head in a pop-up shop on Main Street. It was for the crowdfunding site Kickstarter. I learned about Kickstarter from Jim, who had told me how his kids had used it successfully to raise seed money for some of their projects. I knew the broad strokes about it—how you made a pitch about your new enterprise, and set your fund-raising goals, and after you'd achieved your donation goals, you'd send the donors various gifts depending on their pledge levels. The store promoted free consultations by Kickstarter producers at 1:30 p.m. daily; I signed up for a session on my last day. I got there early, but the person who was going to meet with me was late. I was impatiently about to leave when one of the senior people working the store offered to help me.

Since I was soon to be without a regular paycheck, I was intrigued with the idea of crowdfunding. I told the man that I wanted to raise funds to complete my documentary film. He was respectful and genuinely interested in my project. He walked me through all the intricacies of the website and explained what I needed to do to make my pitch as compelling as possible. As for donor gifts, he said, a DVD of the finished film wasn't going to cut it. Instead, he suggested in-kind hours of professional services.

I called Jim from the hotel that night and told him about my experience. He jumped down my throat, "You don't need funding for the film! You're almost finished with it. However, you know, there may be people on Kickstarter doing fashion lines. Why not use it to request money to fund your manufacturing?"

Jim was absolutely right. Rick and I had the means to fund the preproduction to get my clothing line ready for factory manufacturing, but we needed to find additional funding to do the actual manufacturing. We didn't want to take on equity investors, because I adhered to my father's simple advice about building a successful business—keep overhead low and take on absolutely no outside partners. My mind was going into creative overdrive about all the great gifts we could offer donors, from customized dog tag jewelry and branded camisoles for the lower-level donors to actual finished jackets for the higher-level contributors.

What's more, the Kickstarter representative brought home for me a benefit I would not have immediately recognized. Namely, that the simple act of creating the Kickstarter campaign helped you create all the crucial marketing and sales tools you would need with or without special financing.

"Once you get home," the Kickstarter guru instructed me, "go to our website and get the process started. Here's your password." But this meeting that almost didn't happen had an even larger payoff. I felt a profound shift, knowing for the first time that my clothing design endeavor was real. It was no longer a hobby. *I can do this*, I thought to myself. My creativity that had taken a bashing over the past few months came back roaring. I couldn't wait to get started.

Only a week earlier I had gotten on a plane feeling depressed and on toxic overload from all the stress I'd experienced. Now I was heading home recharged and refreshed with only one last day on the job. On that final day, there was no going-away party, and that was appropriate. It was time to move on, and being at total peace with that was liberating. Tears from employees aside, none of the program or contracting officers stopped by to say good-bye and that, too, was almost a relief. There was no drama and, more importantly, no trauma. I was able to walk out the door without a care. That certainly would never have happened without my perfect little vacation in Park City.

CHAPTER 17

The Phoenix Rises
from the Ashes

Trust me, not having to wake up at 5 a.m. for the daily commute I had taken for seventeen years was no problem. It was shockingly quick how my attachment to that former way of life and all of its trappings disappeared. The only exception, of course, apart from the friends I had made at work, was the sudden absence of a regular paycheck. The anxiety of living off savings for the time being, however, had a silver lining. It made me work that much harder to make my new ventures come to life.

My ideas were organized and itemized on a handwritten, two-page document, with more than seventy objectives for the coming year. Some items were bricks-and-mortar stuff, like finding a local factory that could take Tseneh to the next level. Others were about networking with people I had admired and respected over the years, to let them know that I was open to new opportunities.

More than anything else, the time had come to apply my full energy to endeavors in alignment with my true passions. Part of me still believed that I could have kept my day job and still advanced

Tseneh and the other irons in the fire. But in fact, I was now able to make so much more headway with the things I'd been squeezing into my limited spare time. Things were starting to move so fast that I felt like I was on a rocket ship.

Even the simple act of taking Tseneh from "hobby" status as a DBA ("doing business as Nancy Slomowitz") to a limited liability company (Tseneh Design Group, LLC), with its own checkbook, made it feel real and invigorating. It was no longer a tax write-off; instead, it was an actual business. The only real expenses I had previously were purchases of bolts of fabric and payments to my seamstress to sew the samples; that and the investment I had made in turning my closets into moth-proof fabric storage space. That alone would prove to be a smart choice as things expanded.

As the life I had known for almost two decades so quickly fell by the wayside, I was wonderstruck at how other elements lined up to encourage and embolden me. In almost every direction I turned, there were exciting connections and discoveries. The way things unfolded in Park City was just the beginning—an initiation of sorts into a new life, unbridled from inner and outer constraints, all those fears, insecurities, and old baggage that had kept my creative spirit in virtual lockdown.

On a more personal level, Rick and I had been going through a divorce, which was finalized right when all of these other major changes were happening. What was left in its wake was also amazing, almost otherworldly. If anything, the precious friendship between us felt much stronger in the aftermath than it had during our marriage. Recognizing and embracing the truth about our relationship has clearly been liberating for both of us. And most gratefully, our trust in each other, our extraordinary partnership in business, and our caring support for each other on the deepest levels have remarkably all stayed intact. Maybe *Divorcing Your Husband and Keeping Your Best Friend* should be the title of my next book!

After the loss of the contract, what I also hadn't fully expected or appreciated was the value of the team that still remained, which consisted of Rick, my brother Rich, Ed (a marketing and communications expert), and me. Each in our own way (once we recovered from the jolt of change) welcomed the chance to apply our talents and skills to new ventures. Creating a start-up like Tseneh from scratch was far more stimulating than going to the same job every day as we had done for nearly two decades.

Some vestiges of the day job were important for us to preserve for several good reasons. First and foremost, there was a part of my brain that loved working with numbers and creating order out of chaos. I had enjoyed most aspects of my job and was good at it. What I was not good at was compromising my values and integrity when facing incompetence or mismanagement. The century-plus of combined experience we brought to the occupational table had substantial value. The idea of a new subcontract in the near future at another government agency, which would be limited to the aspects that we excelled at and enjoyed, was worth considering. Most importantly, it would be a way for me to stop whining about how screwed up our government is and to play a new role in helping to solve some of its problems.

Other connections seemed to be coming out of the woodwork with a common voice saying, "How can we get involved and collaborate?" For example, a former boss from the agency we had just left had started his own consulting firm. He was working on cleaning up the bureaucracy and reforming governmental spending, which fit perfectly with what I wanted to do. We immediately began exploring ways of working together.

The University of Maryland University College (UMUC), my alma mater and where I had also set up an endowed scholarship in my father's name, was launching innovative ventures and collaborations to fix university accounting practices. Now that I was a free agent it opened up a whole new level of discussions about their goals. And even the network of academics and business professionals in the Transcendental Meditation movement, with outreach to millions worldwide, was seriously interested in what I was doing and was supportive in helping in any way it could.

All the motley experiences of my life seem to become more valuable as I go out on my new limb—like the old tools from art school that I had kept in my closet for decades, convinced that they would come in handy some future day. No past or present relationship is unimportant. The spirit of doing the right thing, keeping a good reputation, and following the golden rule of treating people as you would like to be treated has proven rewarding in unimaginable ways.

At the time of this writing, Tseneh is in preproduction at a local manufacturing company. Rick and I found it searching online via Makers Row, an invaluable resource that matches designers with suppliers. We called them up, and we made arrangements to go there, about a one-and-a-half hour drive from our home. "These guys can take us to the next level," I told Rick after the meeting. And their enthusiasm was heartfelt, as if they were looking for someone like us who shared our priorities for quality.

"We'll get back to you in two days with a plan and a quote," they told us, and they did.

My sketches, designs, and samples are in the hands of professionals who know what it takes to get a product ready for market. The strategy is what other successful brands have done—first create a high-end line, then go into wider distribution. From getting all the kinks out of the samples, cutting the patterns for large-scale production, and working with a fit model to get the size grading just right, it's a huge job! The owners of the factory love the whole idea of what Tseneh is aiming to do, first for women and down the road for men. They see it as a wave of what needs to happen. From the owners to the workers, it's more than just a paycheck for them; it's a chance to use their skills and talents to do something refreshingly out of the ordinary.

Maybe the story shouldn't end here. Perhaps it would be more inspirational if I were sitting here years later with Tseneh as a fabulously successful brand with my creations in wide distribution in all the stores. But that is not the point of why I've shared my story.

Instead, I want to leave you with the conviction that staying true to the journey and all the exciting course corrections along the way has a bigger payoff than any of us could ever imagine. If we keep exploring the source of our true passion, the outcome will always take care of itself.

Stay tuned . . .

About the Author

In her first book, *Work Zone Madness*, Nancy Slomowitz provides real-world insight into the typical land mines encountered in business and offers solutions for readers to rise above workplace dysfunction.

In her second book, *Exposed*, Nancy chronicles her often unconventional and at times otherworldly journey to find fulfillment beyond career achievements and material success.

Nancy continues her journey at her home in Montgomery County, Maryland.